TOP 10 MIAMI AND THE KEYS

CONTENTS

4

Introducing Miami and the Keys

18

Top 10 Highlights

44

Top 10 of Everything

80

Area by Area

138

Streetsmart

MIAMI AND THE KEYS

INTRODUCING

Early morning at Hollywood Beach

WELCOME TO MIAMI AND THE KEYS

Combining urban chic, tropical beauty, and a distinct Latin American flavor, Miami and the Keys offer sensory delights like nowhere else. Don't want to miss a thing? With Top 10 Miami and the Keys, you'll enjoy the best the region has to offer.

Miami has always forged ahead with its own avant-garde vision. The city has long been a gateway to Latin America and the Caribbean, and the rhythms and flavors of these communities are an integral part of the city's diverse urban tapestry. Little Havana is home to Cuban juice stalls and looming cigar factories, while Little Haiti is a haven of art

Neon-lit bars and hotels in South Beach

galleries and riotous street performances. Miami's coastal location means local life plays out on the beach: the hedonistic heart of South Beach, with its tiki bars, al-fresco clubs, and towering hotels, is the perfect place to see and be seen. And rising above it all are the pastel-hued facades of the Art Deco District and the soaring skyscrapers of Downtown, testament to the city's pioneering architectural identity.

No less captivating is the natural oasis that stretches out just beyond the city's border. The Everglades is a vast natural river system of swamps and wetlands; further south, the Keys are a verdant archipelago of over 10,000 tropical islands strung out in a narrow line. These biodiverse environments seem a world away from the bustle of Miami, their coral reefs, mangrove forests, and teeming swamps harboring an abundance of wildlife. The dizzying contrast between city and sea is just one reason why the region remains so enduringly popular.

So, where to start? With Top 10 Miami and the Keys, of course. This pocket-sized guide gets to the heart of the region with simple lists of 10, expert local knowledge and comprehensive maps, helping you turn an ordinary trip into an extraordinary one.

THE STORY OF MIAMI AND THE KEYS

Miami might be known for its bold 20th-century architecture and neon-lit veneer, but the city and wider region has a rich history, long pre-dating the arrival of European colonists. Here's the story of how it came to be.

First Humans

Humans first arrived in Florida after the last Ice Age and for some 11,500 years were split into small communities. While some roamed the wetlands as nomadic hunter-gatherers, others developed settlements along Florida's rivers, seaboard, and islands.

By the 3rd century BCE, the Tequesta peoples had settled in these regions, their villages thriving for centuries in the subtropical climate.

Contact With Europeans

After sighting Florida in 1513, the Spanish were the first Europeans to colonize the region. By 1565, the Spanish had claimed Florida as a colony, and a Spanish Jesuit mission was established on the north bank of the Miami River in 1567. Though early accounts suggest Spanish residents cultivated a civil relationship with Indigenous peoples, the Tequestas were largely wiped out by the end of the 16th century, due to a plethora of diseases and rising local hostilities.

Seminoles and Slavery

Throughout the 17th and 18th centuries, Spain controlled Florida as its colony, without ever establishing a large settler community in the region. Various Indigenous groups – known as the Seminoles – unified in Spanish-controlled Florida throughout the

The oldest Spanish settlement in Florida

Seminoles during the First Seminole War in the 1800s

1700s. Tensions grew between the Seminoles and settlers from the independent United States to the north in the early 1800s.

Due in part to enslaved peoples in the United States fleeing south – beyond the clutches of the transatlantic slave trade – the US government sought to expand its territory. In 1821, the US purchased Florida from the Spanish as part of the Adams-Onís Treaty; shortly after, in 1845, Florida was officially incorporated to become the 27th state.

The mid-19th century was defined by three Seminole Wars, which arose as a result of the US forcing Indigenous peoples into reservations in the Florida panhandle.

The Birth of Miami

In the mid-19th century, the name "Miami" was used to describe a settlement around Fort Dallas, in reference to the Maiyami, or "big water", people who first settled around nearby Lake Okeechobee. Its small population increased after businessman Henry M. Flagler extended his Florida East Coast Railway from the mainland down to Key West in 1896, and local governors initiated a wave of infrastructural development. To facilitate this building, laborers came from the Bahamas and the Caribbean, with many living in Coconut Grove and Overtown, which quickly became thriving settler communities.

Moments in History

3rd century BCE
The Tequesta peoples settle around Biscayne Bay.

1513
Juan Ponce de León is the first European to sail into Biscayne Bay.

1817
The First Seminole War begins between Indigenous groups and US settlers.

1821
The US purchase Florida from Spain as part of the Adams-Onís Treaty.

1896
The Florida East Coast Railway paves the way for Florida's tourism boom.

1900
New arrivals from the Bahamas populate Coconut Grove.

1904
Mass draining of the Everglades begins in earnest.

1925
Coral Gables is officially incorporated as a city.

1947
The Everglades is officially designated as a national park.

1970
A series of violent drug wars begin between cartels vying for control of the cocaine trade.

2010
New skyscrapers dominate the Miami skyline, testament to the city's role in global trade.

2024
Governor Ron DeSantis endorses Trump for president, marking a distinct divide between the politics of Miami and the wider state.

The Gilded Age

The early 20th century was a period of major economic growth for Miami, with rapidly increasing tourist numbers. Local planners were keen to extend this traffic to the wider region: ambitious (and ecologically destructive) drainage schemes irrevocably transformed the Everglades as a result. The era's optimism was reflected in bold architectural ventures including the planned city of Coral Gables, designed by George Merrick, and a host of Art Deco structures built in the 1920s. For a time, it seemed wealth and imagination were the only limits to success in Miami.

These optimistic investors hadn't reckoned with the region's unpredictable climate, however. The Miami hurricane of 1926 wreaked havoc on the city, and the storm was to prove a harbinger of the coming decades.

Depression and World War II

Florida suffered gravely during the Great Depression of the 1930s, with many investors losing money. Though a small area around Miami Beach was

Damage from Hurricane Andrew in 1992

The tropical bayfront of modern Miami

spared the starker economic effects – it saw a further Art Deco boom in the mid-1930s – the whole region was to encounter greater troubles in the form of World War II. In 1941, the US established military bases in Dade County, the first of dozens to be built across the state.

After the war ended, many soldiers stationed in Florida remained in the state, swelling Miami's population. The end of the war would bring further changes to the region: a new post-war respect for America's beauty led to the creation of the Everglades National Park in 1947, in an attempt to protect America's largest tropical wilderness.

Miami's growing population was bolstered yet further only a decade later, when revolutionary Fidel Castro came to power in Cuba in 1959. Hundreds of thousands of Cubans fled their home country, many enticed by a generous assimilation package offered by the US government. Little Havana became a bustling center of Latin life.

Glitz and Glamor

As the economy soared through the 1970s and 80s, Miami was defined by its hedonism. Crowds of young people came to make the most of the city's glitzy clubs and easy access to illicit drugs. A gateway to Colombia, Bolivia, and Peru, the city became a hub for the cocaine trade, and a series of drug wars erupted between gangs and police.

The end of the 20th century brought additional complications to south Florida. In 1992, Hurricane Andrew caused billions of dollars of damage to the south of the state, and any planned rebuilding was hampered by financial scandals within the state government. These combined factors meant Miami was named the US's fourth-poorest city in 1996.

Miami and the Keys Today

By 2010, Miami had largely recovered from the malaise of the late 1990s, and a wave of construction saw the skyline transformed by soaring skyscrapers. Southern Florida's wealth was still due in large part to tourism, with a stream of global arrivals.

Today, the city's diverse population – over 70 per cent of which is Hispanic – and creative spirit ensure it remains one of America's most exciting destinations. Though Florida's politics has become increasingly divided – due to Trump's second term and the populist platform of governor Ron DeSantis – the Sunshine State's tropical beauty remains undimmed.

TOP 10
EXPERIENCES

Planning the perfect trip to Miami and the Keys? Whether you're visiting for the first time or making a return trip, there are some things you simply shouldn't miss. To make the most of your time – and to enjoy the very best the Sunshine State has to offer – be sure to add these experiences to your list.

1 Take a foodie tour of Little Havana

Cafecito (Cuban coffee), *croquetas*, and hearty Cuban sandwiches: Latin food is the lifeblood of Little Havana. Cuban diners are found on every corner, and companies like Miami Culinary Tours *(www.miamiculinarytours.com)* whisk you through the city's flavors.

2 Book a sunset cruise

Miami's unmistakable skyline and bayfront beauty is best admired from the calm waters of Biscayne Bay. Cruise out around "Millionaire's Row" to see grand and architecturally ambitious – not to mention dizzyingly expensive – properties dotted across lush islets like the Barrier Islands *(p101)*.

3 Relax on the beach

Where sand is concerned, you're spoiled for choice in the Miami area. Lummus Park *(p55)* in South Beach offers the definitive Miami beach scene – think sun loungers, volleyball, and public bodybuilding. For a quieter swim, make for the waters of Bill Baggs Cape Florida State Park *(p84)*.

4 Go shopping

Designer boutiques, bargain-packed outlets, kitsch souvenir shops: shopping is a serious business in Miami. Sawgrass Mills *(p75)* is one of the largest malls in the US (and that's saying something), selling everything you could possibly need and countless things you never will.

5 Explore the Everglades

A vast river system comprising swamps and shimmering wetlands, the Everglades is one of the most fascinating ecosystems in the US. Stroll the flat boardwalk around Corkscrew Swamp *(p43)* or cycle the loop road through Shark Valley *(p42)*.

6 Drive Highway 1

Running all the way from Key Largo to Key West, US 1, the Overseas Highway, traverses 42 bridges, including the Seven Mile Bridge. The route is regarded as one of America's most beautiful, and offers the best way to soak up the majesty of the Keys.

7 Sip a cocktail at a tiki bar

Piña colada, anyone? Countless bars around Miami Beach take the Polynesian concept of the tiki bar and give it a charming Latin spin. Sipping tropical cocktails by the beach is a Miami rite of passage, so put your feet up and indulge in a rum-based tipple.

8 Go diving

Florida's marine environments are every bit as flamboyant as the streets of Miami, and much of the magic takes place beneath the waves. At John Pennekamp Coral Reef *(p121)* you can snorkel out to teeming reefs, meeting local celebrities like the spiny lobster.

9 Lose yourself in Coral Gables

George Merrick's city of Coral Gables *(p32)* is a wonderful architectural fantasy, harking back to Miami's economic boom in the 1920s. Designed mostly in the Mediterranean Revival style, the city is utterly impressive.

10 Visit a local gallery

Miami has always attracted creatives and visionaries. It's no surprise, therefore, that its galleries and museums are packed with outlandish wonders. Pick of the bunch is the Lowe Art Museum *(p34)*, home to almost 20,000 pieces.

ITINERARIES

Exploring sprawling malls, tucking into Cuban dishes, or taking to the waters of the Everglades: there's a lot to see and do in Miami and the Keys. With places to eat, drink, or shop, these itineraries offer ways to spend 2 days and 4 days in the region.

2 DAYS

Day 1

Morning

Begin your Miami adventure with a trip to Bayside Marketplace *(p94)*, a sprawling two-story shopping and entertainment venue right on the banks of Biscayne Bay. Grab a coffee and some breakfast from the gargantuan food court – Miami doesn't do small – before eating overlooking the bay. Then it's time to hit the water. Take a boat tour of Biscayne Bay, marveling at the city's remarkable skyline from the tranquil waters; there's no better way to see the sights. When you're back on dry land, stroll to Downtown *(p92)*, where you can take in the exhibits and gardens at the Pérez Art Museum. Break for a spot of lunch on the terrace of the museum's restaurant.

EAT

A retro diner of epic proportions, Big Pink *(p88)* has more than 200 menu items – from breakfast to snacks. Its signature pink Volkswagen Beetle parked out front only adds to its vintage Miami appeal.

Afternoon

Miami is a smorgasbord of 20th-century architectural styles, but it's particularly associated with Art Deco. To see the liveliest examples of the style, head along Collins and Washington avenues in the Art Deco

Dining al fresco overlooking Biscayne Bay

District *(p24)* – the former is nicknamed the "Capital of Cool" for its abundance of boutiques. Look for distinctive hotels like the Colony, the Beacon, and the Breakwater, designed to resemble ocean liners. Make time for the unique Wolfsonian–FIU museum *(p36)*, home to an eclectic assortment of 20th-century ephemera, from outlandish furniture to icons of graphic design. Finish your day with a stylish meal at Gianni's, housed in the former villa of celebrated designer Gianni Versace *(p23)*.

Day 2

Morning

This morning, you'll make for Little Havana, the heart of Miami's Cuban diaspora. Start the day with a traditional Cuban breakfast at renowned diner Versailles *(p99)*, which proudly calls itself the world's most famous Cuban restaurant. Now, it's time to lose yourself in the neighborhood's crowded streets. Swing past the Little Havana Cigar Factory *(p29)* and the Calle Ocho Walk of Fame *(p29)* – the sidewalk is decorated with the names of Cuban celebrities – before touring the Cubaocho Museum and Performing Arts Center *(p94)*, home to a delightfully tempting rum bar. For lunch, grab a loaded Cuban sandwich from one of the many delis or street stalls.

Afternoon

Take a leisurely walk (or catch the bus) south to Coral Gables *(p32)*, the pioneering planned suburb designed by developer George Merrick. Its winding avenues are lined with pretty villas, and you'll want to spend some time marveling at The Biltmore *(p32)*, one of America's most celebrated hotels. Your final destination is the Vizcaya Museum and Gardens *(p30)*, an elaborate villa fringed by some of the city's finest green spaces. Relax in the gardens, before heading for dinner at Monty's *(montysrawbar.com)*, a bayside hangout in nearby Coconut Grove.

The tranquil Vizcaya Museum and Gardens

4 DAYS

Day 1

Spend your first morning kicking back on the beach, a definitive Miami pastime. Head to Lummus Park *(p55)* at the heart of South Beach, where you can play volleyball, take a dip, or simply soak up the sun. Suitably rested, stroll down Ocean Drive, Miami's most popular thoroughfare, for a lunch at one of the many ocean-facing cafés. Locals often rollerblade or cycle the sidewalks, so why not hire a city bike *(p86)*? South Beach is famous for its lifeguard huts – many sitting between 10th and 16th streets – which are best admired on a short ride down the promenade. When you're ready, make for Española Way, where you can peruse small art galleries and boutiques. Spend a chilled evening nursing a rum runner or two with some snacks – but remember, the party rarely starts before midnight.

DRINK

Española Way is home to some of the best Cuban cocktail and cigar bars in Miami, offering mojitos and jugs of potent sangria.

Day 2

It's time to leave the city and cruise along the beautiful Gold Coast *(p38)*, heading past the eastern beaches up to West Palm Beach. Take the 50-mile (80-km) drive slowly, all the better to soak up the tropical splendor (you can also take the Brightline train if you don't have a car). Your first stop is Dr. Von D. Mizell-Eula Johnson State Park *(p38)*, which offers beautiful views of Port Everglades. Stretch your legs with a walk around the park, before carrying on to Fort Lauderdale, where you can treat yourself to an upscale lunch on Las Olas Boulevard *(p38)*. Your final destination this afternoon is Palm Beach, but you can take a break at the Gumbo Limbo Nature Center; its beautiful boardwalk winds through mangroves and dense swamp-hugging forests. Once you reach Palm Beach, tour the Flagler Museum *(p38)*, an opulent mansion built by entrepreneur William M. Flagler, which houses a number of artistic riches. Finish your day with cocktails and fine seafood at The Breakers *(p150)*, before spending the night in Palm Beach.

Day 3

Today is all about the Everglades *(p42)*. Head south of Palm Beach to join the Tamiami Trail (US 41) which links the Atlantic and Gulf coasts, passing through the center of Everglades National Park. Stop at Shark Valley, where you can walk or cycle the 15-mile (24-km) road, keeping an eye out for dozing alligators. Remember that food options in the Everglades are limited, so bring a packed lunch or stop at one of the roadside diners on the Miami side of Shark Valley. To truly experience the wonders of the park, you'll need to leave terra firma. Big Cypress National Preserve *(p42)* is the perfect place to hire a kayak or canoe. You can spend the afternoon rowing out on the slow-moving waters of the Turner River, the banks home to wading birds including egrets and herons. Drive back to Miami for the evening.

SHOP

Replacing Palm Beach's original main street is Via Flagler, an outdoor shopping plaza featuring a collection of unique boutiques and galleries.

Day 4

Start early today to enjoy the long and beautiful drive down Highway 1 to Key West. As you cruise south through the Keys, stop at Key Largo and Marathon to admire the beauty of Florida's southern tip. These tiny islets are strung out like a jewel across the Florida Straits, and you'll have countless opportunities to stop for coastal walks. In the afternoon, break up the four-hour journey with a dip and a picnic at Bahia Honda State Park *(p121)*. When you arrive in Key West, your first stop is the Hemingway Home *(p40)*, where the famous author lived from 1931 to 1940. If you have time, you can also explore the Mel Fisher Maritime Museum *(p123)*. Watch the sun set over Mallory Square, and end with an infamous "Duval Crawl" through the bars and clubs of Duval Street: the perfect Florida sundowner.

The famous Duval Street in Key West

TOP 10 HIGHLIGHTS

Neon-lit Colony Hotel in the Art Deco District

COLONY
COLONY
HOTEL

EXPLORE THE **HIGHLIGHTS**

There are some sights in and around Miami and the Keys that you simply can't miss, and it's these attractions that make up the Top 10. Discover what makes each one a must-see on the following pages.

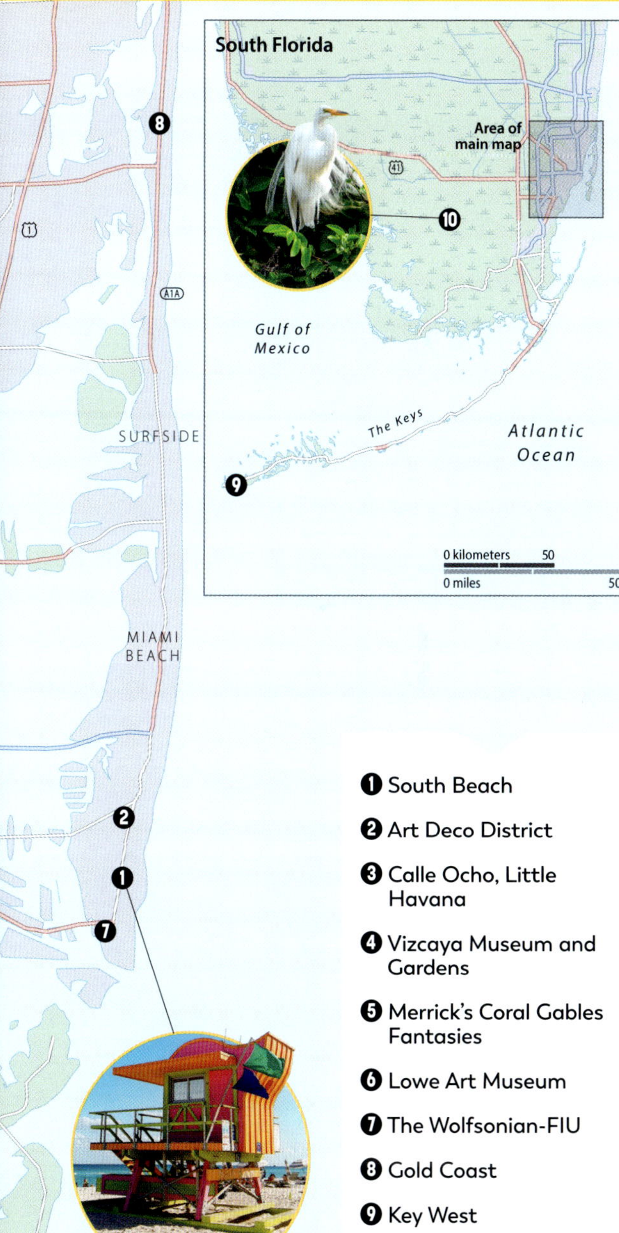

❶ South Beach

❷ Art Deco District

❸ Calle Ocho, Little Havana

❹ Vizcaya Museum and Gardens

❺ Merrick's Coral Gables Fantasies

❻ Lowe Art Museum

❼ The Wolfsonian-FIU

❽ Gold Coast

❾ Key West

❿ The Everglades

1

SOUTH BEACH

H3

SoBe, the nickname for Miami's beautiful South Beach district, was inspired by Manhattan's SoHo. Since the 1980s, the district of South Beach has been a romantic and buzzy area. Today, it is the epicenter of Miami's beach life, with plenty of clubs, cocktail bars, boutiques, restaurants, and stylish hotels.

1 Lincoln Road Mall

Developer Carl Fisher envisaged this pedestrian promenade *(p84)* in 1912. Today, it is a cultural hub with many galleries, restaurants, and shops.

2 Española Way

R3 visit espanolaway.com

This Mediterranean Revival enclave is all salmon-colored stucco, stripy awnings, and red-tile roofs. Built in 1922–5, it was meant to be an artists' colony but soon became an infamous red-light district. It now houses boutiques and offbeat art galleries.

3 Collins and Washington Avenues

R4

These cool cousins of Ocean Drive offer quirky shops and fine Art Deco buildings. Among them is the striking Miami Beach Post Office, with a mural *(p51)* by local artist Charles Hardman.

4 Old City Hall

R3 1130 Washington Ave

With its buff-colored 1920s Mediterranean Revival tower, the Old City Hall is a distinctive SoBe landmark. Its red-tile roof can be seen for blocks around. The building now houses the O Cinema South Beach theater *(o-cinema.org)*.

TOP TIP

Use the ParkMobile app *(parkmobile.io)* to find and pay for parking in South Beach.

South Beach's iconic Ocean Drive

5 SoBe Clubs

Most of South Beach's top clubs *(p89)* are on Washington and Collins avenues, between 5th and 24th streets. Few get going until midnight at the earliest, but before long the party well and truly starts.

6 Big Pink

This all-pink retro diner *(p88)* is a SoBe mainstay. Browse through the morning paper over a full breakfast, or try the special "Big Pink TV Dinner", served on a steel tray.

7 Ocean Drive

This beachfront strip is a popular spot for locals to stroll, skate, and bike. Take in the bright tropical sun, the abundant, candy-colored Art Deco architecture *(p24)*, and the many people-watching cafés.

8 Villa Casa Casuarina

S4 1116 Ocean Dr
vmmiamibeach.com

A Mediterranean Revival-style building, the Villa houses a hotel and an Italian fine-dining restaurant called Gianni's, (advance booking required). Designer Gianni Versace once lived in this mansion.

9 Lummus Park Beach

Much of the sand at this swath of busy park and 300-ft- (90-m-) wide beach *(p55)* was imported. It stretches for ten blocks from 5th Street north.

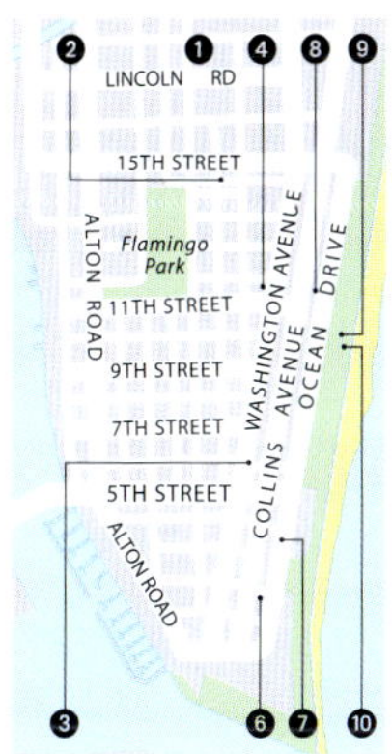

10 Lifeguard Huts

After a hurricane in 1992 destroyed most of the lifeguard stations, several artists were called in to create fun replacements. The best of these stands can be found near Ocean Drive, between 10th and 16th streets.

Clockwise from right **One of the many whimsically designed lifeguard huts in South Beach; patrons enjoying a meal at the popular Big Pink diner**

LGBTQ+ RENAISSANCE

South Beach is a top destination for LGBTQ+ travelers. The LGBTQ+ scene took off here in the late 1980s and 1990s; the LGBTQ+ Visitor Center *(p67)* opened in 2010, and Miami Beach Gay Pride Parade debuted in 2012. Pride flags dotted throughout indicate queer-friendly businesses. The festivals, all-night events, and parties draw crowds from around the world.

ART DECO DISTRICT

H3 Art Deco Welcome Center: 1001 Ocean Dr at 10th St; mdpl.org

South Beach's Art Deco District consists of more than 800 beautifully preserved buildings. These structures embody Miami's unique interpretation of the Art Deco style, which took the world by storm in the 1920s and 1930s. Florida's take on it is often called Tropical Deco, with buildings designed to look like ocean liners (Nautical Moderne) or styled with curving, streamlined features (Streamline Moderne).

The Colony Hotel's neon sign

1 Colony Hotel

S4 736 Ocean Dr colonymiami.com

Perhaps the most famous of the Art Deco hotels along Ocean Drive, primarily because of its blue neon sign, Colony Hotel has featured in many movies and series.

2 Beacon Hotel

S4 720 Ocean Dr beaconsouthbeach.com

The abstract decoration above the ground floor of the hotel has been brightened by a contemporary color scheme, an example of "Deco Dazzle," introduced by designer Leonard Horowitz in the 1980s.

3 Breakwater Hotel

S4 940 Ocean Dr breakwatersouthbeach.com

This Streamline Moderne hotel was built in 1939. It features blue-and-white racing stripes and a striking central tower that recalls a ship's funnel. The tower is most beautiful at night, when it is lit up in neon blue.

DRINK

Mango's Tropical Café *(p90)* is florid and steamy, and always bustling with activity. Sip on a mojito here as you listen to live music.

4 Gabriel Hotel

R4 640 Ocean Dr hilton.com

Designed by famed architect Henry Hohauser in 1937, the former Celino Hotel became the Gabriel in 2021, but retains its Nautical Moderne theme.

5 The Tides

S3 3901 Ocean Dr tideshollywoodbeach.com

An Art Deco masterpiece, the Tides resembles a luxury ocean liner. Completed in 1936, it was designed by the architect Lawrence Murray Dixon – a big name in the Art Deco history of South Beach. At 161 ft (49 m), it was briefly the tallest building in Miami.

6 Essex House

Erected in 1938, this stark, white building *(p149)* closely resembles a ship, with "porthole" windows and awnings that look like railings. It isn't difficult to find this landmark; just look for the neon-lit spire.

Cycling past the Waldorf Towers

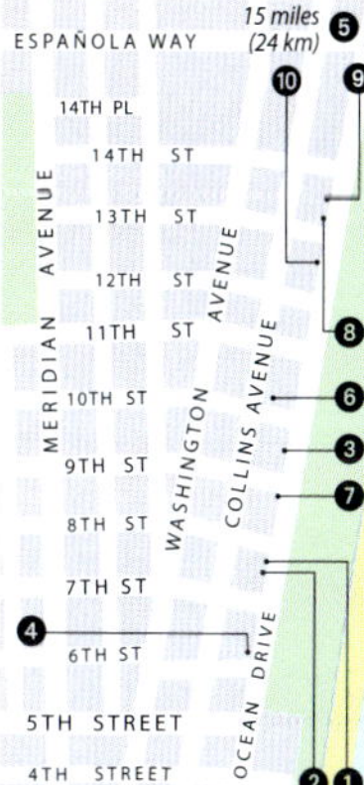

7 Waldorf Towers

S4 860

Ocean Dr waldorf towersmiami.com

Here stands one of the first examples (1937) of Nautical Moderne, where the style is taken to one of its logical extremes with the famous ornamental lighthouse on the hotel's roof. Fantasy towers were the stock-in-trade for Deco architects.

8 Cardozo Hotel

A late Hohauser work (1939), this place *(p148)* is a Streamline masterpiece, in which the detail of traditional Art Deco is replaced with rounded sides, aerodynamic racing stripes, and other expressions of the modern age. The hotel is now owned by the Cuban American singer Gloria Estefan.

9 Cavalier Hotel

S3 1320

Ocean Dr cavalier southbeach.com

A traditional Art Deco hotel, the Cavalier provides a contrast to the later Cardozo next door. Where the Cardozo emphasizes the horizontal and nautical, this facade is starkly vertical and temple-like. The temple theme is enhanced by vertical stucco friezes, which recall the abstract, serpentine geometric designs of the Aztecs and other Meso-American cultures.

Facade of the Cavalier Hotel

10 Leslie Hotel

S3 1244

Ocean Dr leslie hotel.com

The Leslie (1937) is white and yellow with gray accents. Inside are shades of turquoise and pink.

Tropical Deco Features

1. Neon
Used mostly for outlining architectural elements, neon lighting, in a range of colors, came into its own with the Tropical Deco style.

2. Ice-Cream Colors
Most Deco buildings here were originally white, with a bit of painted trim; the present-day rich pastel palette "Deco Dazzle" was the innovation of Miami designer and Barbara Baer Capitman collaborator Leonard Horowitz in the 1980s.

3. Nautical Features
There's no better way to remind visitors of the ocean and its pleasures than with portholes and ship railings. Some of the buildings resemble beached liners.

4. Curves and Lines
The suggestion of speed is the core of the Streamline Moderne style – it is an implicit appreciation of the power of technology.

5. Tropical Motifs
These motifs include Florida palms, panthers, orchids, and alligators, but especially birds, such as flamingos and cranes.

Art Deco mural in the Colony Theatre

6. Stylized, Geometric Patterning
This was a nod to the extreme modernity of Cubism, as well as the power and precision of technology, a key part of Bauhaus precepts.

7. Stucco Bas-Relief Friezes
These sculptural bands provided Art Deco designers with endless possibilities for a wonderful mix of ancient and modern motifs and themes for the buildings.

8. Fantasy Towers
Many Art Deco buildings try to give the viewer a sense of something mythical – towers that speak of far shores or exalted visions – and that effectively announce the hotel's name, as well.

9. Chrome
Nothing says "modern" quite like a cool and incorruptible silver streak of chrome. This material is used as detailing on and within many Deco buildings.

10. Glass Blocks
Used in the construction of many Deco walls, the glass blocks give a sense of lightness in a part of the country where indoor-outdoor living is a year-round lifestyle.

Typical highlighting on the McAlpin hotel

THE STORY OF TROPICAL DECO

The Art Deco style took the world stage following the 1925 International Exhibition in Paris, synthesizing all sorts of influences, including Art Nouveau's flowery forms, Bauhaus, Egyptian imagery, and the geometric patterns of Cubism. In 1930s America, Art Deco buildings reflected the belief that technology was the way forward, absorbing the speed and edginess of the Machine Age as well as the fantasies of science fiction and even a tinge of ancient mysticism. The thrilling new style was just what was needed to counteract the gloom of the Great Depression and give Americans a coherent vision for the future. In Miami, the style was exuberantly embraced and embellished with the addition of numerous local motifs, becoming "Tropical Deco." Its initial glory days were not to last long, however. Many hotels became soldiers' barracks in World War II and were torn down afterward. Fortunately, Barbara Baer Capitman *(p47)* fought a famous battle to preserve these buildings. The Miami Beach Historic District was designated in 1979.

TOP 10 ARCHITECTS

1. Henry Hohauser: Gabriel, Colony, Cardozo, Essex, Webster, Taft
2. Albert Anis: Waldorf, Avalon, Majestic, Abbey
3. Anton Skislewicz: Breakwater, Kenmore
4. L. Murray Dixon: Tiffany, Fairwind, Tudor, Senator, St. Moritz
5. Igor B. Polevitsky: Shelborne
6. Roy F. France: Cavalier
7. Robert Swartburg: Delano, The Marseilles
8. Kichnell & Elliot: Carlyle
9. Henry O. Nelson: Beacon
10. Russell Pancoast: The Bass

Buick Oldtimer at the Avalon Hotel

CALLE OCHO, LITTLE HAVANA

K3

Little Havana has been the core of Miami's Cuban community since the 1960s, when Cuban immigrants first started settling here. The area's heart is Southwest 8th Street, better known by its Spanish name, Calle Ocho. Its liveliest stretch, between SW 11th and SW 17th avenues, is best explored on foot, but other attractions beyond can be reached by bus, trolley, or ride share.

LITTLE HAVANA: AN AMERICAN STORY

Named a National Treasure in 2017, this is Miami's most iconic neighborhood and, over time, has become a symbol of America's rich immigrant history. Political exiles, fleeing the turmoil caused by the Cuban revolution, flocked here in their thousands during the 1960s, creating this colorful and vibrant enclave.

1 Plaza de la Cubanidad

At the plaza is a bronze map of Cuba and an enigmatic quote by Cuban revolutionary hero José Martí.

2 Cuban Memorial Boulevard Park

The site of the Brigade 2506 Memorial *(p46)* honors the Cuban Americans who died in the Bay of Pigs invasion of Cuba in 1961. Other memorials pay tribute to Antonio Maceo and José Martí, who fought against Spanish colonialism.

3 Little Havana Visitors Center

If you're looking for Cuban souvenirs, this is the store for you *(p98)*. Shop for cigars, art, and coffee, as you sample the homemade ice cream.

4 José Martí Park

Named after the famous poet and patriot, this tranquil oasis was dedicated in 1985 to the Cuban struggle for freedom. In the 1980s, the site became a Tent City for many homeless Cuban refugees.

Mural in the heart of Little Havana

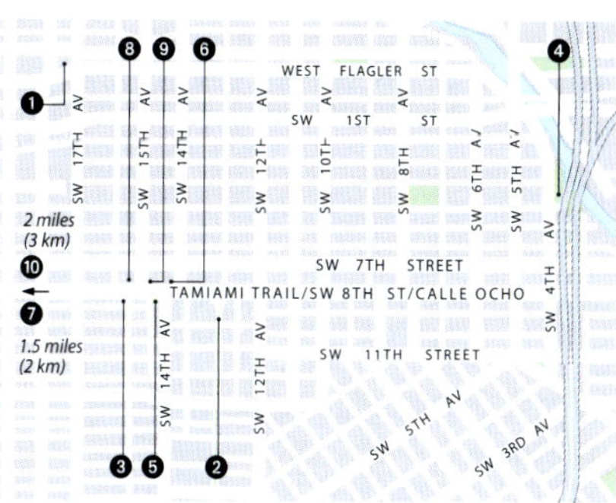

5 Domino Park

For decades, Cubans have gathered at the corner of SW 15th Avenue to match wits over games of dominoes, making it an important meeting spot.

6 Calle Ocho Walk of Fame

Little Havana's version of Hollywood's Walk of Fame, this lovely stretch features pink marble stars embedded in the sidewalks, honoring Cuban celebrities like salsa singer Celia Cruz as well as famous Latin Americans with ties to South Florida.

7 Woodlawn Park North Cemetery

Here lie the remains of two Cuban presidents, including Gerardo Machado, as well as the Nicaraguan dictator Anastasio Somoza.

8 Little Havana Cigar Factory

1501 SW 8th St
10am–7pm daily (to 6pm Sun) littlehavanacigars.com

This inviting store and lounge resembles a 1950s cigar club.

9 Cubaocho Museum and Performing Arts Center

This hybrid space *(p94)* is both a rum cocktail bar, with live music, and a museum that celebrates local Cuban culture with its exhibitions and events. It also serves as a popular venue for retired locals to meet up and play dominoes.

10 Versailles

No trip to Miami is complete without a visit to this legendary restaurant *(p99)*. It's a Cuban version of a classic diner, with a delicious menu of Latin classics, mirrors on every wall and a constant friendly hubbub.

Clockwise from right **Stars on the Calle Ocho Walk of Fame; entrance to the Little Havana Cigar Factory; Domino Park, a popular spot to watch dominoes in action**

VIZCAYA MUSEUM AND GARDENS

L6 3251 South Miami Ave 9:30am–4:30pm Wed–Mon Thanksgiving & Christmas Day vizcaya.org

Excessively opulent and undeniably grand, the Vizcaya Museum is the former villa and estate of millionaire industrialist James Deering. Completed in 1916, the rooms are a blend of styles from Renaissance to Neo-Classical. Its formal garden is one of the city's most impressive, combining the features of Italian and French gardens with Florida's tropical foliage.

1 French Rococo Reception Room

The assemblage is a mix of styles, but the look is of a salon under the 18th-century French King Louis XV. The tinted-plaster ceiling is from a Venetian palace.

2 Neo-Classical Entrance Hall and Library

The mood in these English Neo-Classical-style rooms is more somber than other parts of the house. They were inspired by the work of Robert Adam.

3 Italian Renaissance Living Room

Being the largest room in the house, the living room includes many notable pieces, such as a 2,000-year-old marble Roman tripod, a tapestry depicting the *Labors of Hercules*, a 15th-century Hispano-Moresque rug, and a Neapolitan altar screen.

4 Italian Renaissance Dining Room

Inspired by a Renaissance banquet hall, the dining room features a 2,000-year-old Roman table, complete with a full set of 17th-century chairs, and a pair of 16th-century tapestries.

DEERING'S DREAM

James Deering was keen for his winter residence to provide a sense of family history as well as luxury. Thus he bought and shipped bits of European pomp and reassembled them on this ideal spot right by the sea.

5 Breakfast Room

On the upper floor, the breakfast room features a fireplace and offers fine views of the gardens.

6 Empire Bathroom

Deering's elaborate bathroom has marble walls, silver plaques, and a canopied ceiling. The bathtub was designed by Deering to run either fresh or salt water from the Biscayne Bay.

7 Rococo Music Room

Arguably the loveliest room in the house, the Rococo Music Room is lit by a striking chandelier featuring multicolored glass flowers. The room has an exquisite Italian harpsichord dating from 1619, a dulcimer, and a harp.

8 East Loggia

This portico frames magnificent views out over the sea and of the quaint stone breakwater known as the Barge. Carved in the shape of a large ship, it provides a perfect foreground to Key Biscayne, which lies just off the coast.

9 Formal Gardens

The villa's elaborate formal gardens, extending over 10 acres (4 ha), are a highlight of the site. The fountains of gracefully carved stone, statuary, and cleverly laid-out formal plantings offer ever-changing vistas. The Secret Garden and playful Maze Garden showcase great artistry.

Coral-stone exterior of the museum

Ornate Rococo-style Music Room

10 Swimming Pool Grotto

This swimming pool, which partially extends below the living room, creates a unique space reminiscent of homes along the canals of Venice. The walls of the pool are decorated with seashells and depictions of marine life, while the ceiling features beautiful frescoes.

Vizcaya Museum and Gardens Plans

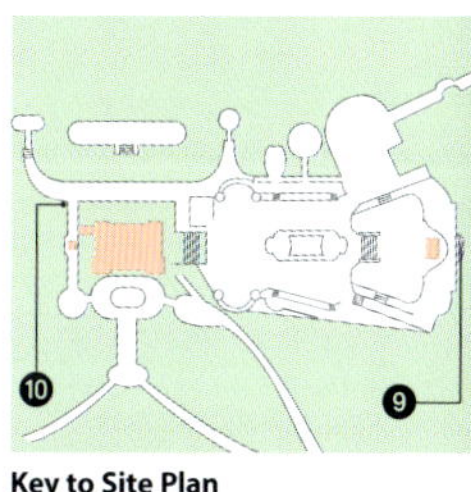

Key to Site Plan

Museum

Gardens

Key to Floor Plan

First floor

Second floor

5

MERRICK'S CORAL GABLES FANTASIES

G3

Coral Gables is a separate city within Greater Miami. Aptly described as the "City Beautiful", its swanky homes line avenues shaded by giant trees, alongside a network of canals. Regulations ensure that new buildings use the same architectural vocabulary advocated by George Merrick when he planned the city in the 1920s. He created a place with a unique architectural identity that has lost none of its aesthetic impact.

1 The Biltmore

George Merrick's 1926 masterpiece has been refurbished and burnished to its original splendor and remains one of the most stunning hotels *(p151)* in the country. It served as a military hospital during World War II and a veteran's hospital until 1968. A 315-ft- (96-m-) near replica of Seville Cathedral's Giralda tower rises from the hotel's imposing facade. Inside, Herculean pillars line the grand lobby, while the terrace offers views of one of the largest hotel swimming pools in the US.

2 Congregational Church

Coral Gables' first church built by Merrick in Spanish Baroque style is a replica of a church in Costa Rica. It has an elaborate bell tower and portal.

3 Florida Pioneer Village

These are imitations of the early plantation and colonial homes built by Florida's first aristocrats. The style incorporates Neo-Classical, columned porches with the stucco walls of tropical tradition.

MERRICK THE VISIONARY

Merrick's dream was to build an American Venice. The project was the biggest real estate venture of the 1920s, costing around $100 million. The hurricane of 1926 then the Wall Street crash of 1929 left his city and his dream incomplete, but what remains is proof of his imagination.

4 French Normandy Village

The most homogeneous of all the villages at Coral Gables, this is all open timberwork, white stucco, and shake (cedar) roofs. Little alcoves and gardens here and there complete the picture-postcard look.

Majestic facade of The Biltmore

Stunning Venetian Pool in Coral Gables

5 Venetian Pool

The claim that this is one of the most beautiful swimming pools *(p107)* in the world is a fair one. Incorporating grottos and waterfalls, it was fashioned from a coral rock quarry in 1923 by Merrick's associates, Phineas Paist and Denman Fink.

6 Italian Village

The typical country type of Italian villa, with its red-tile roof and painted stucco walls, can be found here. Many later constructions have carried on the theme, so the original Merrick creations are almost lost in the mix.

7 Chinese Village

An entire block has been transformed into a walled enclave of Chinese-inspired architecture. The curved, glazed-tile roofs are painted in vibrant colors. Some also feature motifs of dragons and bamboo.

8 French City Village

Here you'll find nine *petits palais* in the French style, looking as if a city block of Paris has been airlifted to the US.

9 French Country Village

Seven mansions are built in various styles typical of the French countryside. Some have open timber, stone, red brick, and shake (cedar) roofs, while others resemble the classic grange.

10 Dutch South African Village

This collection of homes embodies the high-peaked facades and scrolls of typical Dutch architecture, along with white stucco walls and red roofs associated with the Mediterranean. The style evolved as Dutch settlers adapted to African climes.

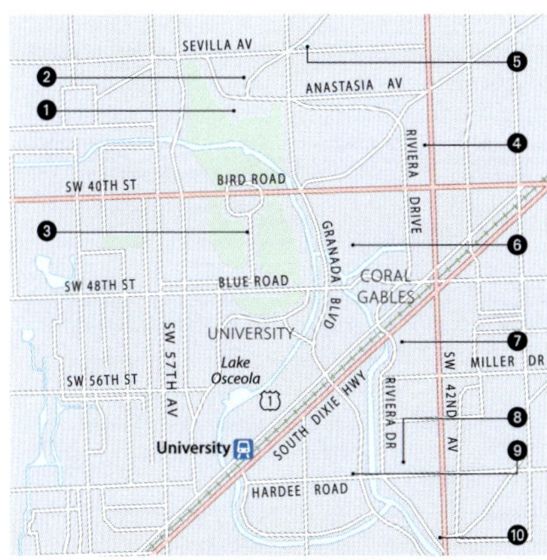

6

LOWE ART MUSEUM

F3 · 1301 Stanford Dr · 10am–4pm Wed–Sat · lowe.miami.edu

One of Miami's premier art venues, the Lowe was founded in 1950, and built in 1950–52 thanks to a donation from philanthropists Joe and Emily Lowe. Around 19,500 pieces showcase many of the world's most important artistic traditions, including those of the Renaissance and Baroque eras. The permanent collection incorporates artifacts from over 5,000 years of human history.

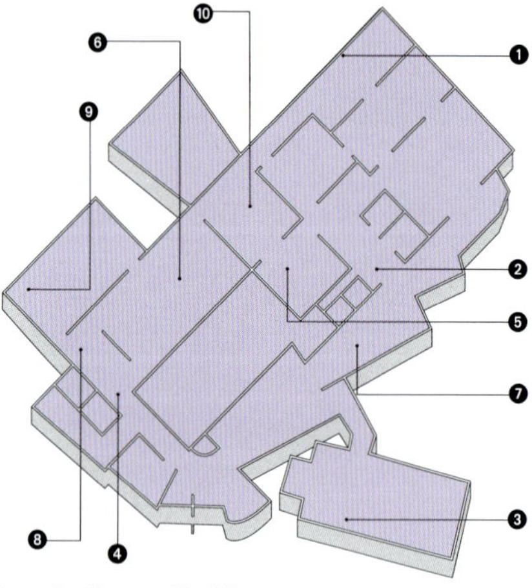

Lowe Art Museum Site Plan

1 Native American

A Seminole shoulder bag, beautifully embroidered using thousands of tiny, colored-glass trade beads, is the pride of this collection. Also on show are Najavo, Hopi, and Apache art forms, which include masks, textiles, pottery, and brightly painted wooden *kachina* dolls.

2 Ancient American

The collection covers all eras and areas, from about 1500 BCE to the 16th century. A silver disk engraved with complex iconography from 14th-century Peru is a rare piece, and the colorful wood figurine from Colombia is notable.

3 Contemporary Glass and Studio Arts

This stunning $3.5 million glass collection features works by Dale Chihuly, Richard Jolley, and William Carlson.

4 Egyptian

This excellent collection includes Coptic textiles, and there is also a jewel-like portrait sarcophagus mask, intended to resemble the features of the deceased. There are some medieval manuscripts on display, too.

5 Asian

One of the museum's strongest collections, with superb Chinese ceramics, as well as bronze and jade pieces, and other ceramics from Neolithic times

Pre-Columbian wood figurine

EAT

A local favorite, the Titanic Brewing Company *(p113)* serves up tasty seafood, with live music, and great handcrafted ale.

Exhibits from the African collection

to the 20th century. There is also classic, folk, and tribal art from India.

6 Latin American

Notable holdings of 20th-century art by Hispanic artists include works by Fernando Botero of Colombia, Arnaldo Roche-Rabell of Puerto Rico, and Cuban-born Carlos Alfonzo.

7 17th-Century to Contemporary European and American

Some extraordinary works from this collection on display include *Football Player* by Duane Hanson, *Americanoom* by Chryssa, *Le Neveu de Rameau* by Frank Stella, *Portrait of Mrs Collins* by Thomas Gainsborough, *Modular Painting in Four Panels* by Roy Lichtenstein, and *Rex* by Deborah Butterfield.

8 Greco-Roman

Classical sculpture is represented by marble carvings, including a bust of a Roman matron. The 6th-century BCE black-figure krater depicting Artemis, Leto, and Apollo is noteworthy.

9 Renaissance and Baroque

This exquisite collection of mostly paintings includes works by Battista Dossi, Tintoretto, Jordaens, Lucas Cranach the Elder, and Palma Vecchio.

10 African

While focusing on the sub-Saharan region, this collection also showcases art from across the African continent. Highlights include the 16th-century bronze ring of the Yoruba people, a Nok terra-cotta figure, and items from Elpe or Ngbe society.

MUSEUM GUIDE

There is no particular order in which you are expected to view the collections at the museum, which is located at the campus of the University of Miami. Keep in mind that several of the galleries are given over to temporary exhibitions.

Admiring artworks in the Renaissance and Baroque galleries

THE WOLFSONIAN–FIU

R4 1001 Washington Ave, Miami Beach 10am–6pm Wed–Sun (to 9pm Fri) Public hols wolfsonian.org

Set in a 1920s building, this museum was once a storage site, where Miami's wealthy stored their valuables while traveling north. It now houses a remarkable collection of around 200,000 objects spanning decorative and fine arts, including books, posters, sculptures, and furniture, primarily from North America and Europe.

1 Entrance Hall

The massive ceiling supports reflect the Mediterranean Revival style of the facade and are original. So are the terra-cotta floors, the woodwork over the doors leading to the elevator vestibule, and the rough stucco walls. All of the ornamental cast stone was done by hand.

2 Ceiling, Chandeliers, and Brackets

These decorative features come from a 1920s Miami car showroom.

3 Art Deco Mailbox

To the left of the elevator is a 1929 Art Deco bronze mailbox, originally from New York Central Railroad Terminal in Buffalo.

TOP TIP

Download Bloomberg Connects (*wolfsonian.org/visit/bloomberg connects*), a free digital guide.

4 Harry Clarke Window

This literature-themed stained-glass window was created in 1926–30 for the League of Nations' International Labor Organization in Geneva, Switzerland.

5 Wooden Staircase

Designed by Wharton Esherick in 1935, this fine piece of modern woodcraft, fashioned from pine and steel, came from the Curtis Bok residence in Gulph Mills, Pennsylvania.

6 Fountain

Positioned under a skylight, this fountain was made from an elaborate Deco window grille from the Norris Theater in Pennsylvania.

Stunning Harry Clarke Window

Clockwise from above **Mediterranean Revival-style facade of the museum; cast aluminum sculpture, *The Wrestler*; "frozen fountain" in the museum lobby**

Composed of over 200 gilded and glazed terracotta tiles, the richly floral decoration belies the careful geometrical structure of the piece.

7 The Wrestler

A symbol of The Wolfsonian–FIU, this brawny, nude, life-sized form by American sculptor Dudley Talcott is made of aluminum, perhaps the classic metal of 20th-century modernity.

MUSEUM GUIDE

The Wolfsonian–FIU is a museum and a design research institute at the Florida International University. Three floors are offices and storage and are not usually open to the public. Your tour should begin outside, progress to the Entrance Hall, then up the back elevator to floors 5, 6, and 7.

8 Temporary Exhibits

Much of the space is used for special exhibits exploring themes of the modern age. The Wolfsonian is a leading authority on propaganda art, showing how savvy designers have used the science of psychology to their advantage to create highly persuasive images for businesses and governments.

9 Mediterranean Revival Building

The Spanish Baroque-style relief around the main entrance is a striking feature. Its bronze flagpoles and finials date from 1914.

10 Bridge Tender's House

Just north of The Wolfsonian's entrance is this remarkable 1939 Art Deco-style building, now known as the Josephine Baker Pavilion. This striking

The Wolfsonian–FIU Floor Plan

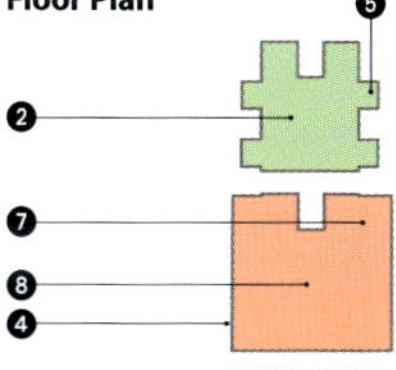

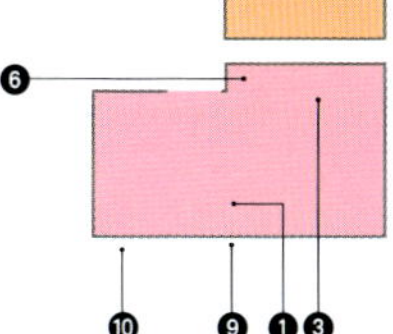

Key to Floor Plan

- First Floor
- Fifth Floor
- Sixth Floor
- Seventh Floor

stainless-steel, hexagonal structure was rescued from demolition, rebuilt, and donated to the museum in 1993. Today, it often serves as a venue for contemporary art installations.

GOLD COAST

D2–D4

One of the best ways to enjoy Florida's east coast is by traveling along the Gold Coast between West Palm Beach and Miami. This scenic 50-mile (80-km) road hugs the beach, passing nature preserves and historic neighborhoods. Though an easy day trip, it's worth taking your time to admire the attractions along the way. Much of the route can also be toured via public transport by taking the Brightline intercity train and local buses.

Vibrant walls and decor at Bonnet House

1 Flagler Museum

1 Whitehall Way, Palm Beach flaglermuseum.us

This mansion was Henry M. Flagler's wedding gift to his third wife, Mary Lily Kenan, who was half his age and an heiress herself. The trappings of royalty are everywhere, including the 18th century Louis XV commode.

2 Norton Museum of Art

Perhaps Florida's finest museum of art *(p49)*, the Norton has more than 8,200 Impressionist, American, Chinese, and European works of art.

3 Las Olas Boulevard, Fort Lauderdale

A colorful shopping mall, Las Olas Boulevard is also the departure point for river cruises. Nearby, Fort Lauderdale's main street is home to shops and restaurants *(p74)*.

4 Worth Avenue, Palm Beach

Stretching across four blocks from Lake Worth Beach to the Atlantic Ocean, this avenue *(p75)* is Palm Beach's best-known social hub.

5 Dr. Von D. Mizell-Eula Johnson State Park

8am–sunset daily floridastateparks.org

Home to a beach once designated for African Americans during segregation, this long barrier island offers superb views of the busy Port Everglades. Today, it is a popular destination for the LGBTQ+ community.

EAT

Enjoy lunch specials, appetizers, handmade pasta, flavorful drinks, and sumptuous desserts at Noodles Panini *(noodlespanini.com)* in Fort Lauderdale.

6 Bonnet House

Built in 1920, this period home is full of the personality of its creators, Frederic and Evelyn Bartlett. They were both artists, as is evident from the highly original murals and the somewhat eccentric tropical gardens.

7 Gumbo Limbo Nature Center

This informative center has a boardwalk that winds through mangroves and hammocks (raised areas) in Red Reef Park *(p58)*. It takes its name from the gumbo

Bustling Hollywood Beach Broadwalk

limbo tree, which is notable for its distinctive red peeling bark.

8 Boca Raton Museum of Art

501 Plaza Real, Boca Raton **W boca museum.org**

Located inside the beautiful Mizner Park in downtown Boca Raton, this art museum hosts world-class exhibitions. Its impressive permanent collection includes 19th-, 20th-, and 21st-century art, sculpture, and photography.

9 The Broadwalk

This famous stretch of Hollywood Beach runs for 2.5 miles (4 km) from Jefferson Street to Sheridan. It is lined with shops, bars, and restaurants, including the popular beach shack, Riptide Tiki Bar. The beach is also a lovely spot for families to just sit back and relax.

10 The Breakers

The aura of America's Gilded Age (1877–96) is still evident in this stylish abode, from the frescoed Italianate ceilings to the crystal chandeliers *(p150)*. It is the third hotel to be built on this site, the first two having burned down.

Grand interiors at The Breakers

ALL THAT GLITTERS

Here, all that glitters might just be gold! The Gold Coast may be named for the gold doubloons that Spanish galleons used to transport along the intracoastal waterways, but these days the term is used more for the golden lifestyle of the many millionaires and billionaires who have winter homes here.

9

KEY WEST

A6 Chamber of Commerce, 510 Greene St; keywestchamber.org

The southernmost settlement in the continental US, Key West is a city like no other. It sits on a tiny island, or key, measuring approximately 4 miles (6.5 km) in length and about 2 miles (3 km) in width. Though the tourism industry has brought significant changes to the area, it retains a uniquely eccentric character, and many writers, artists, and free thinkers are among its self-named Conch (pronounced "konk") inhabitants.

1 Custom House Museum

281 Front St 10am–5pm daily kwahs.org

Located inside the imposing old Customs House, this museum of art and history exhibits paintings of some of the island's eccentrics and notables, along with accounts of historic life.

2 Mallory Square

Every evening at sunset, the fun-loving citizens of the self-styled "Conch Republic" throw a party in this square, complete with entertainers.

3 Audubon House

205 Whitehead St 9:30am–4:15pm daily audubonhouse.org

This house offers visitors a glimpse into mid-19th-century island life.

4 The Hemingway Home

907 Whitehead St 9am–5pm daily hemingwayhome.com

Ernest Hemingway lived from 1931 to 1940 in this Spanish colonial-style coral-rock house. Above the carriage house is the room where the novelist penned several works. Descendants of his six-toed cats still roam.

5 Key West Cemetery

The tombs are raised to avoid flooding, as the soil is mostly hard coral rock. Droll epitaphs include "I told you I was sick" on the tomb of a hypochondriac.

6 Mel Fisher Maritime Museum

200 Green Street melfisher.org

This engaging museum is dedicated to all kinds of

Lighthouse towering over Key West

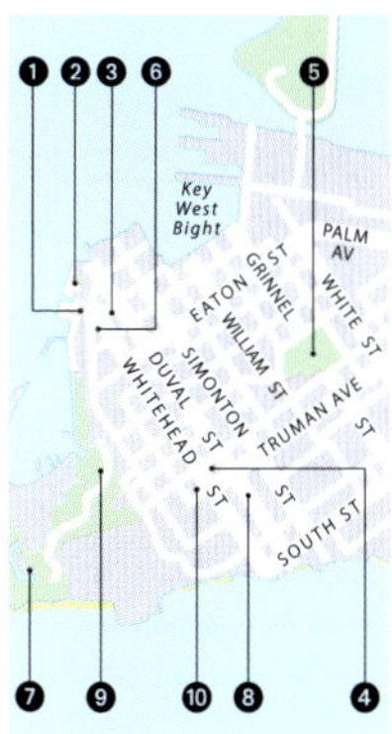

shipwreck treasures, including items retrieved from Spanish galleons.

7 Fort Zachary Taylor Historic State Park

8am–sunset daily floridastateparks.org

This 1866 fort is now a military museum, showcasing Civil War artifacts.

8 Duval Street

The main street of Old Town is the place to attempt the legendary "Duval Crawl" – stopping in at all of the 100 or so bars, pubs, and clubs that line Duval Street and its environs.

9 Bahama Village

An archway over Petronia Street at Duval marks the entrance to this neighborhood, where the first Black Bahamian settlers arrived in the 19th century. Head to the Bahama Market and Blue Heaven restaurant for a slice of island culture.

10 Lighthouse

938 Whitehead St kwahs.org

Opened in 1848, this lighthouse could beam light 25 miles (40 km) out to sea. At its base, the keeper's cottage now houses a museum.

THE BUSINESS OF WRECKING

The coral reef around Key West has been responsible for many shipwrecks. In the 1700s, Bahamians patrolled the reef to salvage shipwrecks for trade goods. This scavenging, known as "wrecking", grew so popular that in 1825 an act of the US Congress decreed that only US residents could have salvage rights.

Bars and clubs lining Duval Street

THE EVERGLADES

C4

Comprising one of the planet's most fascinating ecosystems, the Everglades is a shallow river system of swamps and wetlands, where the waters can take a year or more to meander from the Kissimmee River, northwest of Miami, into Florida Bay. At least 45 plant varieties are unique to this area. It is also home to over 350 kinds of bird, 300 types of fish, and many mammal species.

1 Big Cypress Swamp

Oasis Visitor Center; 239 695 2000

This shallow wetland is a range of wet and dry habitats determined by slight differences in elevation. It is home to several hundred species, including the endangered Florida panther.

2 Ah-Tah-Thi-Ki

Ah-Tah-Thi-Ki means "a place to learn." This museum *(p48)* focuses on Seminole culture and history. It houses more than 180,000 artifacts to explore, and has a fantastic library.

3 Royal Palm Visitor Center

305 242 7700

Both Anhinga and Gumbo Limbo trails begin at the Royal Palm Visitor Center, the site of Florida's first state park.

4 Shark Valley

This area, only 17 miles (27 km) from the western edge of Miami, has a 15-mile (24-km) loop road that you can

Cape Coral
Naples
Boca Raton
Coral Springs
Big Cypress Swamp
Miami
Kendall
Homestead
Flamingo
Key Largo
441
75
41
1
2
3
4
5
6
7
8
9
10

Exploring the Anhinga Trail

travel by bicycle or on a narrated tram ride. It ends at a tower that affords great views.

5 Flamingo

Guy Bradley Visitor Center; 239 695 2945

This outpost was damaged by Hurricane Irma in 2017. However, sportfishing, camping, and canoeing are possible. In 2023, the Guy Bradley Visitor Center reopened along with a new lodge and restaurant.

6 Mahogany Hammock

Near Flamingo is one of the park's largest hammocks (fertile mounds), where a trail meanders through dense tropical growth. This is home to colorful tree snails and the largest mahogany tree in the country.

7 Everglades National Park

nps.gov/ever

The park features trails for walking and cycling, elevated boardwalks, tours, canoe rental, and accommodation. It also offers many boat trips.

8 Tamiami Trail (US 41)

Its name a portmanteau of Tampa and Miami, this was the first road to open up the area by linking the Atlantic and Gulf coasts. It passes pioneer camps, such as Everglades City and Chokoloskee, which mark the western edge of the Everglades.

9 Fakahatchee Strand

floridastateparks.org

This is one of Florida's wildest areas, a 20-mile (32-km) slough (muddy backwater), noted for its rare orchids and the largest stand of native royal palms in the US.

PRESERVING THE EVERGLADES

The Everglades evolved over a period of more than six million years, but humans almost destroyed its fragile balance in less than 100. In the 1920s, the Hoover Dike closed off the area's main water source, Lake Okeechobee. Environmentalist Marjory Stoneman Douglas *(p47)* reversed the situation. Today, work continues on building levees to help retain the area's moisture.

10 Corkscrew Swamp

corkscrew.audubon.org

A boardwalk here leads through various habitats, including old cypress full of nesting birds.

Clockwise from right **Heron taking flight; observation tower at Shark Valley; airboat tour in the Everglades National Park**

TOP 10 OF EVERYTHING

Al-fresco dining on Lincoln Road, Miami Beach

Van Dyke Cafe

HISTORIC SITES

1 Vizcaya Museum and Gardens

James Deering's opulent monument with its rich artistic traditions has become Miami's most beloved social and cultural center *(p30)*.

2 Ancient Spanish Monastery

Built in 1133–41 in Segovia, Spain, this monastic building *(p101)* was bought by William Randolph Hearst in 1925 and shipped to New York. The parts were reassembled here in 1952.

3 Charles Deering Estate

James Deering's half-brother built this residence *(p116)* for himself. The original 19th-century house, Richmond Cottage, was restored after being damaged by Hurricane Andrew in 1992.

4 Coral Gables Merrick House

This is the house *(p110)* where the Merrick family lived in the early 1900s and where master builder George Merrick grew up. The contrast between the modest surroundings of his home and the spectacle of his grandiose dreams is fascinating.

5 Coral Castle

This monument *(p115)* to unrequited love was built single-handedly from coral rock, using tools assembled from automobile parts. Latvian architect Edward Leedskalnin sculpted most of the stones 10 miles (16 km) away in Florida City and transported them – also by himself – to their present site. At that time, land was cheap (he bought his one-acre plot for just $12 in 1920) and the area was sparsely populated.

6 Brigade 2506 Memorial

W bayofpigsbrigade2506.com

R2

Little Havana's Eternal Flame and monument garden remembers those who died in the Bay of Pigs, trying to reclaim Cuba from Fidel Castro in 1961.

7 Indian Key Historic State Park

This Florida Keys island preserve *(p123)* is rich in history. In the 1830s, a community of wreckers briefly thrived here before being destroyed in the Second Seminole War.

8 The Barnacle

Built in 1891, this is Dade County's oldest house *(p109)*, which cleverly uses

Admiring the sculpted stones at Coral Castle

ship-building techniques to make it stormproof as well as comfortable, allowing for Florida's steamy climate.

9 Stranahan House

D3 335 SE 6th Ave, near Las Olas stranahanhouse.org

Fort Lauderdale's oldest house was built originally in 1901 as a trading post for the Seminoles. The handsome two-story riverside house is furnished with period antiques, but it is the photos that best evoke the past, such as Stranahan trading alligator hides, otter pelts, and egret plumes with the local Seminoles. Such prizes were brought in from the Everglades in dugout canoes.

10 Holocaust Memorial

R2 1933–45 Meridian Ave, South Beach holocaustmemorialmiamibeach.org

Miami has one of the largest populations of Holocaust survivors in the world, so this stunning monument has extra poignancy. Sculpted by Kenneth Treister and completed in 1990, the centerpiece is a huge bronze forearm bearing a stamped number from Auschwitz. The arm is thronged with nearly 100 life-sized figures in positions of suffering. The surrounding plaza has a tunnel lined with the names of Europe's concentration camps, a graphic pictorial history of the Holocaust, and a granite wall inscribed with the names of thousands of victims.

Bronze forearm, Holocaust Memorial

TOP 10 MOVERS AND SHAKERS

Marjory Stoneman Douglas

1. Marjory Stoneman Douglas (1890–1998)
An environmentalist, who saved the Everglades from development.

2. Betty Mae Tiger Jumper (1923–2011)
She became the first and only female chief of the Seminole Tribe in 1967, and founded the tribe's newspaper.

3. Roxcy Bolton (1926–2017)
Miami-based civil rights activist, with a focus on women's rights.

4. Manny Diaz (b. 1954)
This Cuban American politician served as mayor of Miami from 2001 to 2009.

5. Ruth Bryan Owen (1885–1954)
Florida's first female US Representative in Congress, and later the first woman appointed as a US ambassador.

6. The Deering Brothers
James *(p30)* and Charles *(p116)* built homes that are now major attractions.

7. William Brickell (1817–1908)
One of the first men to take advantage of the Homestead Act of 1862.

8. Barbara Baer Capitman (1920–90)
Capitman was the driving force behind the movement to save the area's Art Deco hotels *(p27)*.

9. Julia Tuttle (1849–98)
The dynamic pioneer who convinced Henry Flagler to extend his railroad down to Miami, in 1896.

10. Chief Jim Billie (b. 1944)
This Seminole chief was responsible for bringing wealth to his people by building casinos on reservations.

MUSEUMS

1 Cubaocho Museum

Learn more about Little Havana's history and culture at this small, yet informative, museum and art gallery *(p94)*. Cuban culture has been a key factor in Miami's identity since the 1950s, a legacy explored through revolving exhibits of Cuban art, an old-fashioned café, a bar serving stellar mojitos and live Cuban arts performances.

2 HistoryMiami Museum

M2 101 W Flagler St 10am–5pm Wed–Sat, noon–5pm Sun historymiami.org

Starting as far back in prehistory as 12,000 years, the museum slips swiftly through the millennia to reach Spanish colonization, Seminole culture, extravagance in the "Roaring Twenties," and Cuban immigration in more recent years.

3 The Wolfsonian-FIU

The perfect complement to the Art Deco District, this museum and design research institute *(p36)* has a wealth of modern design exhibits.

4 Naomi Wilzig Erotic Art Museum

R3 Mezzanine level 1205 Washington Ave 11am–6pm daily (to 11pm Fri–Sun) weam.com

An extensive collection of erotic art from around the world, valued at a whopping $10 million.

5 Ah-Tah-Thi-Ki Seminole Indian Museum

C3 34725 W Boundary Rd, Clewiston ahtahthiki.com

This excellent museum, on the Big Cypress Indian Reservation, features Seminole artifacts, such as pottery and beautiful clothing. The Green Corn Ceremony is also explained, including the games, music, dance, and costumes involved. A nature trail leads through the cypress canopy, where signs explain the use of certain flora in Seminole culture.

6 Jewish Museum of Florida

With its stained-glass windows and Deco details, the former synagogue itself is as fascinating as the

Interior of the historic Jewish Museum of Florida

exhibits it houses. The museum *(p85)* is dedicated to telling the story of the 230-year Jewish presence in Florida.

7 Mel Fisher Maritime Museum

Immerse yourself in the romance of long-lost, booty-laden shipwrecks at this fascinating museum *(p123)*.

8 Lowe Art Museum

This is one of Miami's top art museums *(p34)*, featuring works from European, American, Chinese, Pre-Columbian, and Indigenous cultures.

9 Norton Museum of Art

D2 1450 S Dixie Hwy, West Palm Beach norton.org

One of South Florida's finest museums, the Norton Museum of Art displays works by Europeans, such as Goya, Rembrandt, Renoir, Picasso, and Americans including O'Keeffe and Pollock. Highlights include an impressive array of artifacts from China, featuring ceramic figures of animals and courtiers from the Tang Dynasty (7th–10th centuries CE). The museum also houses modern sculptures by Brancusi, Degas, and Rodin, alongside an excellent collection of photography and contemporary art.

10 Pérez Art Museum Miami

Besides impressive temporary shows, the museum's permanent collection *(p93)* focuses on art since the 1940s, and includes artistic works by Frankenthaler, Gottlieb, Rauschenberg, and Stella. It's set in lovely gardens.

Exquisite Art Deco facade of the Wolfsonian–FIU

TOP 10 CONTEMPORARY COLLECTIONS

1. Margulies Collection
591 NW 27th St
Excellent collection of photography, sculpture, video, and installations.

2. Nina Johnson
6315 NW 2nd Ave
A gallery of one of Miami's top dealers featuring new as well as known artists.

3. Institute of Contemporary Art
61 NE 41st St
Displays works by emerging as well as internationally renowned artists.

4. Bernice Steinbaum Gallery
2101 Tigertail Ave
Steinbaum moved her art gallery from NYC to Miami in 2000.

5. Artspace/Virginia Miller Galleries
169 Madeira Ave
Historically significant Latin American art, paintings, and photography.

6. Locust Projects
297 NE 67th St
Specializing in artistic innovations and experimental new art.

7. Rubell Museum
1100 NW 23rd St
Works by modern artists, including Haring, Koons, Basquiat, and Cuban artist José Bedia.

8. Cernuda Arte
3155 Ponce de Leon Blvd
Cuban art from all periods.

9. Fredric Snitzer Gallery
1540 NE Miami Ct
Features Latin American and avant-garde Cuban contemporary art.

10. Wynwood Walls
2516 NW 2nd Ave
A cutting-edge project brings the world's greatest graffiti artists to Miami.

Graffiti art at Wynwood Walls

ARCHITECTURE

Historic Freedom Tower in the heart of Miami

1 Freedom Tower

A soaring edifice *(p92)* inspired by the famous belfry of Seville's vast cathedral, La Giralda is home to Miami Dade College's Museum of Art and Design.

2 Art Deco District

South Beach's Art Deco District *(p24)* is home to some of the finest examples of Art Deco architecture. By saving the district from demolition, not only was South Beach transformed but it also inspired a national movement to preserve historic structures.

3 Atlantis on Brickell

M5 · 2025 Brickell Ave

Built by the renowned architecture firm Arquitectonica in 1982 and soon thereafter one of the stars of *Miami Vice*, this building is known for its unique "skycourt" – a "hole" high up in its facade. The "hole" is an ingenious 37-ft (11-m) cube cut out of the building's center, at the 12th floor. A red spiral staircase, a palm tree, and a Jacuzzi draw your attention to it in a delightful way.

4 The Biltmore and Coral Gables Congregational Church

Facing each other across gardens, these two structures *(p32)* are the heart of George Merrick's contribution to "the City Beautiful".

5 Fontainebleau Hotel

Designed by architect Morris Lapidus, this landmark *(p149)* defines the Miami Modern Architecture (MiMo) style: sweeping lines, colors, and inlaid marble floors with the trademark bow-tie motif.

6 Ingraham Building

N2 · 25 SE 2nd Ave, at Flagler St, Downtown

This Renaissance-Revival beauty is an unmissable landmark, and it evokes all the glamor of the 1920s boom era.

7 Estefan Enterprises

R5 · 420 Jefferson Ave, Miami Beach

A playful building that takes the frivolity of Deco several steps further, with a free-form green-wave tower slicing through a cool blue cube, evoking both sea and sky.

8 1111 Lincoln Road

Q2 · 1111 Lincoln Rd, at Alton Rd, South Beach

This unique open-air structure, completed in 2010 by Swiss architectural firm Herzog & de Meuron, looks like a precarious stack of cards.

Beautifully illuminated Miami Tower

9 Miami Tower

I. M. Pei's striking take on the ziggurat theme, so often used in Art Deco, looks for all the world like a stepped stack of CDs in various sizes. The tower *(p94)* is especially appealing at night when lit up with vibrant colors.

10 Key West Old Town

This small island *(p40)* has one of the US's largest collections of 19th-century structures. About 4,000 buildings, mostly houses, embody the distinctive local style. Many architectural features take their cues from elements used on ships, such as roof hatches to allow air circulation. A unique innovation is the "eyebrow" house, with second-floor windows hidden under a front porch roof overhang, providing shade in the heat.

Bustling street in charming Key West Old Town

TOP 10
MURALS AND MOSAICS

1. Bacardi Building
2100 Biscayne Blvd
A Miami landmark, this building has distinctive blue-and-white tile murals with a floral theme, designed by Brazilian muralist Francisco Brennand.

2. Ladies in White
Calle Ocho (SW 8th St) & 15th Ave, Little Havana
This mural was created by local street artist Daniel Fila, also known as Krave Art.

3. The Good Wall
982 Calle Ocho (SW 8th St) Little Havana
Alley of murals that change regularly.

4. Miami Beach Post Office
1300 Washington Ave, South Beach
The classy Deco rotunda of the old post office has a triptych mural of Ponce de León and Indigenous peoples.

5. Coral Gables City Hall
405 Biltmore Way
Denman Fink created the mural on the bell tower's interior. The one above the stairs is by John St. John.

6. Culmer Overtown Branch Library
350 NW 13th St
Local artist Purvis Young painted the "Everyday Life" mural here in 1984.

7. Welcome to Miami Beach
770 Arthur Godfrey Rd, Miami Beach
A postcard on the side of The Roosevelt Theatre by the artist Lebo.

8. The Society of the Four Arts
Four Arts Plaza, Palm Beach
See allegorical murals from 1939.

9. Wyland Whaling Walls
201 William St, Key West
An undersea world of whales and other cetaceans is featured here.

10. Bahama Village
Thomas St at Petronia St, Key West
A charming mural evokes daily life in the Bahama Village neighborhood.

PARKS AND GARDENS

1 Flamingo Gardens

D3 3750 South Flamingo Rd, Davie/Fort Lauderdale flamingogardens.org

These gardens started out in 1927 as a weekend retreat for the citrus-farming Wray family. There's an aviary featuring an array of Florida birds, including the comical roseate spoonbill and, of course, the flamingo. A native butterfly and nectar-plant conservatory opened in 2023.

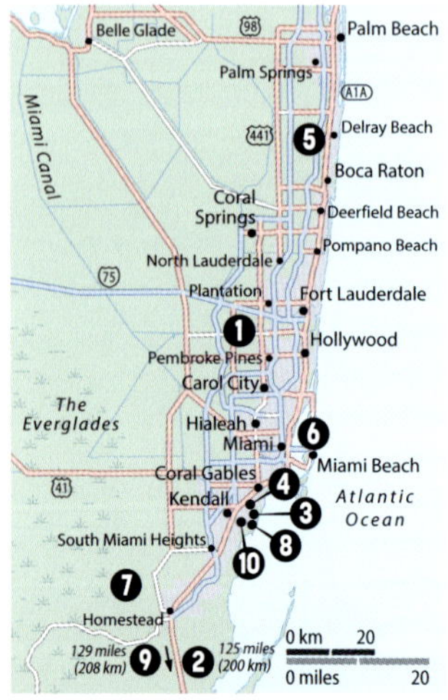

2 Key West Tropical Forest & Botanical Garden

A6 5210 College Rd, Key West keywest.garden

Established in 1936, this is the only frost-free, subtropical botanical garden in the continental US, and is home to endangered species. Trails and boardwalks wind through the 15-acre (6-ha) reserve, showcasing flora native to Florida Keys, Cuba, and the Caribbean. It's known for its "champion trees", among them a saffron plum and cinnamon bark. With two wetland habitats and two dedicated butterfly gardens, it's also a haven for migratory birds and tropical butterflies.

3 Fairchild Tropical Botanic Garden

One of the best of South Florida's ravishing tropical gardens *(p116)* dotted with artificial lakes and a large collection of rare plants.

4 Tropical Audubon Society

F4 5530 Sunset Dr

With a mission to restore Florida's ecosystems, visitors are invited to explore the Doc Thomas House, the Steinberg Nature Center, and acres of lush hardwood hammock habitats and pine rockland.

Flock of pink flamingos at the Flamingo Gardens

5 Morikami Museum and Japanese Gardens

D3 4000 Morikami Park Rd, Delray Beach morikami.org

Blossoming from a Japanese colony founded here in 1905, the Yamato-kan villa is surrounded by formal Japanese gardens of various ages: a Heian (9th- to 12th-century) *shinden*-style garden, a paradise garden emulating those of the 13th–14th centuries, rock gardens, a flat garden, and a modern romantic garden.

6 Miami Beach Botanical Garden

R2 2000 Convention Center Dr, Miami Beach mbgarden.org

This 3-acre (1.2-ha) oasis flaunts a Japanese Garden, Edible Garden (with papayas, pineapples, and the like), and a palm garden. After admiring the orchids and flowering trees, take a walk along the promenade that shadows Collins Canal.

7 Fruit & Spice Park

Located in the Redland District south of Coconut Grove, this is the only tropical botanical garden *(p115)* of its kind in the United States. The non-native plants are grouped by country of origin, and the tropical climate here sustains over 180 varieties of mango, 40 of banana, and 15 of jackfruit. The vast, lush park also houses the largest bamboo collection in the US. In the gift store you'll find imported fruit products, including dried and canned fruit, juices, jams, teas, and unusual seeds.

8 Montgomery Botanical Center

This nonprofit botanical center *(p116)*, accessible by appointment only, holds a vast collection of plants from across the globe.

9 Nancy Forrester's Secret Garden

A6 518 Elizabeth St, Key West

Lose yourself in this impossibly lush acre of land just a block off Duval Street. Intensely beautiful, the garden exudes a sense of peace and contentment. The ravishing varieties of flora – orchids, bromeliads, rare palms – and the well-loved parrots put any visitor at ease.

10 Pinecrest Gardens

This thoroughly enjoyable place features over 1,000 kinds of tropical plant, an art gallery, and an amphitheater for concerts and shows. There are also plenty of activities here *(p64)* for children.

Water lilies at the Pinecrest Gardens

BEACHES

1 South Pointe Park Beach

R6

Though not well known for its beaches, South Pointe Park's northern part is frequented by surfers, and you can watch cruise ships gliding in and out of the Port of Miami. It's also great for walks, and there's a fitness course, an observation tower, and picnic spots.

2 Haulover Park Beach

H1

Located just north of Bal Harbour, Haulover has been spared the sight of high-rise development. Noted for its clear blue waters, the dune-backed beach lies along the eastern side of the park *(p102)*. To the north is a clothing optional stretch – the only nude beach in the county.

3 Crandon Park

One of several South Florida beaches *(p84)* rated among the top ten in the US, this one is on upper Key Biscayne.

4 Matheson Hammock Park Beach

G4

North of Fairchild Tropical Botanic Garden, this beautiful 100-acre (40-ha) park was developed in the 1930s by Commodore J. W. Matheson. It features the human-made Atoll Pool, a saltwater swimming pool encircled by sand and palm trees and flushed naturally by the nearby Biscayne Bay. The tranquil beach is popular with families and enjoys warm, safe waters surrounded by tropical hardwood forests. Other attractions include walking trails through the mangrove swamp, a full-service marina, a snack bar set in a historic coral rock building, picnic pavilions, and nature trails.

Lighthouse at the Bill Baggs Cape Florida State Park

5 Bill Baggs Cape Florida State Park

Home to a historic 19th-century lighthouse, this pristine beach *(p84)* is located at the southern tip of Key Biscayne.

6 Hobie Island Beach and Virginia Key Beach

H3

While Hobie Beach is popular with windsurfers, Virginia Key – neighbor to Key Biscayne and similarly shrouded in Australian pines – has no residents and few visitors. Under Old South segregation, it was the only Miami beach African Americans were allowed

Lifeguard house at Crandon Park beach

to use. Once you walk through the vegetation, the 2-mile (3-km) beach here is fine and relatively empty. Both are excellent for children due to the warm bay waters, but Virginia Key has deep waters and possible undertow.

7 Sunny Isles Beach

More noteworthy for its 1950s tourist-resort kitsch than for its rocky sand, this developing strip *(p101)* is popular with older tourists, as well as surfers and sailors. The souvenir shops and hotels that fringe the beach indulge in striking architectural fancies and mementos. You'll find the majority of stores on Collins (A1A) between 175th and 193rd streets.

8 Lummus Park Beach

S3 1130 Ocean Drive

This stretch of sand – broad, long, and well-maintained – is, for many, the epitome of South Beach. During holiday season, you'll see hordes of sunbathers, some with boom boxes blasting, others just leisurely catching the rays. The more active play volleyball, do gymnastics, and, of course, take to the waves.

Panoramic view of Lummus Park Beach

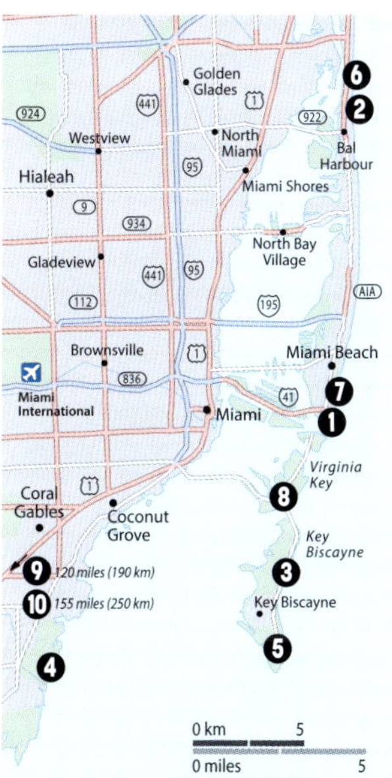

9 Bahia Honda State Park

With two award-winning beaches, Calusa and Sandspur, Bahia Honda *(p121)* is celebrated for its perfect white sands, abundance of water-sports, and tropical forests.

10 Key West Beach

A6

Key West's modest beaches are strung out along the south of the island, stretching from Fort Zachary Taylor Historic State Park in the west to Smathers Beach in the east. The latter is the largest and most popular, but locals favor the former because it's less crowded. For convenience, the beach at the bottom of Duval Street, at the Southernmost Point in the US, is fine, friendly, and offers several good refreshment options.

SPORTS AND OUTDOOR ACTIVITIES

1 Cycling

This is an excellent way to explore South Beach, Key Biscayne, or Key West. Rental shops abound, and there are a good number of excellent bike trails in the Everglades, too.

2 In-line Skating

Gliding along on little wheels is probably the number one activity for the perennially tanned of South Florida. Down on flaunt-it-all South Beach, you can rent in-line skates or get fitted for your very own pair.

3 Golf

You'll get endless opportunities to play golf throughout South Florida, making it a premier golfing-holiday destination. Many larger resorts have their own courses, too, but one of the best in the Greater Miami area is Crandon Golf Course, which is the only public course on Key Biscayne.

4 Volleyball

On every beach in South Florida, you'll find volleyball nets and likely team members ready to go. This is the quintessential beach sport, where taking a tumble in the sand is part of the fun.

5 Fishing

Florida is a hotspot for anglers from all over the world. There are a number of companies, including Reward Fishing Fleet *(fishingmiami.com)* and AWS Charters *(305 304 2483)*, that organize deep-sea fishing excursions. For good freshwater fishing, you should head to Amelia Earhart Park or Lake Okeechobee. Good Times Key West *(goodtimeskeywest.com)* and Fishing Headquarters *(fishheadquarters.com)* are worthwhile options offering a range of fishing experiences, from two-hour excursions to multi-day trips.

6 Swimming

Miami and the Keys are home to some of the most beautiful beaches in the US. Head to Bahia Honda State Park *(p121)* for pristine sandy beaches where you can enjoy the warm, clear blue waters of the Atlantic Ocean and Florida Bay.

Kayaking across the waters at Key Largo

7 Boating and Kayaking

Strike out on your own in a kayak and explore the colorful waters around the Keys, or the mangrove creeks off Florida Bay. Alternatively, you could enjoy an ecotour of the diverse marine life and some of the best birding in the country with Blue Planet Kayak *(blue-planet-kayak.com)*.

8 Tennis

South Floridians love this game, and there are public and private courts everywhere. Key Biscayne is the top choice, while the Miami Open is held at Hard Rock Stadium every March.

9 Jet-Skiing and Parasailing

Florida's extensive coastline and inland waterways offer plenty of opportunities for jet-skiing and parasailing. In Miami, the placid intracoastal waterways are suitable for both, but it's the Keys that have the best conditions for these adventure sports, especially Key West. Book a session with Sunset Watersports *(sunsetwatersportskeywest.com)* or Fury Water Adventures *(furycat.com)* to enjoy these thrilling watersports.

10 Surfing and Windsurfing

Miami has good prevailing winds and both calm and surging waters – so there is plenty of scope for good surfing and windsurfing. The Keys tend to be good for windsurfing only, as the surrounding reefs break the big waves.

Playing volleyball on one of South Florida's beaches

TOP 10 SPECTATOR SPORTS

1. Baseball
Two-time world champions Miami Marlins play Major League Baseball at LoanDepot Park *(501 Marlins Way)*.

2. Jai Alai
The lively game played at Casino Miami *(3500 NW 37th Ave)* originated in the Basque Country and was introduced to the US in the early 1900s through Cuba.

3. Football
Football is hugely popular in Miami and across Florida. Miami's NFL contender, the Miami Dolphins, play their home games at the Hard Rock Stadium *(347 Don Shula Dr)*.

4. Soccer
The Chase Stadium *(1350 NW 55th St, Fort Lauderdale)* hosts Miami's top MLS team, Inter Miami CF.

5. NASCAR racing
Founded by Sanchez, Homestead Miami Speedway *(1 Speedway Blvd)* hosts several big events every year.

6. Tennis
The Miami Open, held at the Hard Rock Stadium *(347 Don Shula Dr)*, is one of the world's biggest non-Grand Slam tournaments.

7. Polo
Popular around Palm Beach County, including at the National Polo Center *(3667 120th Ave S, Wellington)*.

8. Basketball
Miami Heat, who compete in the Eastern Conference of the NBA, call the Kaseya Center (601 Biscayne Blvd) home.

9. Ice Hockey
Ice hockey is popular in Miami, and the local team, the Florida Panthers, play their home games at the Amerant Bank Arena *(1 Panther Parkway, Sunrise)*.

10. The Cognizant Classic
This pro-golf tournament is held at the PGA National Resort and Spa *(Palm Beach Gardens)* every year between February and March.

SNORKELING AND DIVING

1 Looe Key National Marine Sanctuary

Accessible from Bahia Honda State Park, this coral dive site *(p124)* offers the nearest snorkeling opportunities to Key West.

2 Biscayne National Park

Closer to Miami than John Pennekamp, this location *(p117)* has many good snorkeling possibilities. You'll find vivid coral reefs to dive among, and mangrove swamps to explore by canoe.

3 John Pennekamp Coral Reef State Park

While the mangrove swamps and tropical hammocks in the park's upland areas offer a unique experience, it is the coral reefs and diverse marine life that attract visitors. This park *(p121)* also provides some of the best snorkeling in the world. Visitors can rent boats, take a glass-bottomed boat tour, or opt to scuba dive.

Christ of the Abyss statue, John Pennekamp Coral Reef

4 Key Biscayne Parks

Both Crandon and Bill Baggs Parks *(p84)* have great areas for snorkeling, in Miami's cleanest, clearest waters.

5 Key West Waters

A6

Take the plunge right off the beach at Fort Zachary Taylor Historic State Park, or join an expedition out to the reefs that lie around this island. Plenty of trips are offered by local companies, most of them taking three to four hours in total, including at least an hour and a half of reef time. These excursions usually depart several times daily, running until early afternoon.

6 Bahia Honda State Park Waters

The beautiful, sandy beach of Bahia Honda *(p121)* in the Keys – often lauded as one of the best beaches in the US – has excellent waters for swimming and snorkeling. Equipment rentals are available here.

7 Red Reef Park

D3 1400 N Ocean Blvd, Boca Raton Noon–4pm Mon, 9am–4pm Tue–Sun myboca.us/2573/Our-Parks

Boca Raton is famous for its extensive and beautifully maintained parks, and this offers some of the area's best beaches and snorkeling. An artificial reef can provide hours of undersea viewing and is suitable for youngsters. The Gumbo Limbo Nature Center is just across the street.

8 Islamorada

C5

Halfway along the Keys, Islamorada is a superb base for snorkeling and diving trips. The nearby Crocker and Alligator reefs provide habitats for a wide variety of marine life. The shipwrecks of the *Eagle* and the *Cannabis Cruiser* are home to gargantuan amberjack and grouper.

9 Fort Lauderdale Waters

D3

Fort Lauderdale has been awarded Blue Wave Beaches certification for its spotless sands and crystal clear waters, which make for superior underwater viewing. Many of the most interesting parts of the three-tiered natural reef system here are close to the shore, although most require a short boat ride to get to. In addition, more than 80 artificial reefs have been built to enhance the growth of marine flora and fauna in the area. Sea Experience (*seaxp.com*) is just one of several companies organizing thrilling snorkeling and scuba trips off this coastline.

10 Dry Tortugas National Park

Found about 70 miles (110 km) west of Key West, these seven islands and their surrounding waters make a fantastic park (*p133*). The snorkeling sights are exceptional, due to the shallow waters and abundance of marine life. You can snorkel directly off the beaches of Fort Jefferson or go to the wreck of the *Windjammer*, which sank on Loggerhead Reef in 1907. Tropical fish, goliath grouper, and lobster can be spotted.

Diving in waters off Fort Lauderdale

WALKS, DRIVES, AND CYCLING ROUTES

1 Everglades Trails

There are several roads for exploring the Everglades: I-75 or Alligator Alley; Highway 41 or the Tamiami Trail; or the less-developed road (No. 9336) from Florida City. Off all of these roads, you'll find several opportunities for great excursions into the wild.

2 Coconut Grove

Always lively, usually with a young crowd, this area of Miami south of Downtown has a great buzz and is ideal for exploring on foot. As well as shops, outdoor restaurants, and cafés, live bands often play in CocoWalk.

3 Calle Ocho

The main walkable part of Little Havana *(p28)* lies along SW 8th Street, between about 11th and 17th avenues. The interesting spots are quite spread out around the neighborhood, and most of them are best found by driving, then exploring on foot.

4 Hollywood Broadwalk

Starting some 15 miles (24 km) north of South Beach, the Hollywood Beach Broadwalk runs for 2.5 miles (4 km) along the Atlantic shore. The promenade makes for a pleasant stroll or bike ride as it is lined with stores, local bars, and cafés on one side, and golden sands on the other.

5 Palm Beach

Begin your walk at Worth Avenue on the beach at Ocean Blvd. Stroll west and check out as many of the fabulous shops as you dare. Continue on to Addison Mizner's pink palace, Casa de Leoni (No. 450), then take Lake Drive north to Royal Palm Way. Visit the Society of the Four Arts, then continue north to the Flagler Museum. Finally, go east along Royal Poinciana Way and south to The Breakers.

6 Key West Old Town

The only sensible way to get around Key West *(p40)* is either on foot or by bike; there's so much detail to take in and, besides, parking is usually a problem here. A planned tour can be fine, but it's just as good to walk wherever inspiration leads.

7 Art Deco District

With some 800 Tropical Deco wonders to behold, you can hardly miss it; just walk or bike along Ocean

Cycling along Miami's famous Ocean Drive

Drive, and Collins and Washington avenues between about 5th and 22nd streets *(p24)*.

8 Rickenbacker Trail

H3–H4

This 8.5-mile (13-km) paved cycling trail begins south of Downtown Miami and travels the length of Key Biscayne along a dedicated bike lane, taking in ocean views and palm-lined beaches. Starting from Brickell Avenue at Alice Wainwright Park, cycle across the William M. Powell Bridge to Virginia Key, stopping at Hobie Island Beach Park for views of Miami's skyline. Continue across Bear Cut Bridge to Key Biscayne, passing Crandon Park and ending at Bill Baggs Cape Florida State Park and Lighthouse.

9 Miami to Key West

D4–A6

There are great sights along this drive, like the giant lobster at the Rain Barrel. Stop to have a seafood meal on the water. Other attractions include parks and nature preserves, such as Bahia Honda State Park.

10 Routes North

If driving north from Miami, take the Gold Coast Highway A1A – it makes the time spent worthwhile, rewarding the traveler with both natural beauty and the elegant neighborhoods of the Gold and Treasure Coasts.

Palm-fringed shore of Hollywood Broadwalk

TOP 10 ROADSIDE DINERS AND FOOD STOPS

1. Mrs. Mac's Kitchen, Key Largo
C5 99336 Overseas Hwy
No-frills diner famed for its fresh seafood and homemade chili.

2. Sal's Ballyhoo's, Key Largo
C5 97860 Overseas Hwy
Conch house from the 1930s that features a Friday-night fish fry.

3. Alabama Jack's, Key Largo
D5 58000 Card Sound Rd
Tasty conch fritters and live music since the 1950s, on Highway 905A.

4. Hungry Tarpon, Islamorada
C5 77522 Overseas Hwy
Enjoy scenic views and tuna tacos, cracked conch and Thai-style mahi fish fingers at this waterfront restaurant.

5. The Seven Mile Grill, Marathon
B6 1240 Overseas Hwy
Well known for its delicious conch chowder, beer-steamed shrimp, and key lime pie since 1954.

6. No Name Pub, Big Pine Key
The oldest pub *(p63)* in the Keys, known for its dollar bill smothered walls and great thin-crust pizzas.

7. The Village Grill & Pump, Lauderdale-By-The Sea
D3 4404 El Mar Dr
Atmospheric place for seafood, steaks, and great cocktails on Highway A1A.

8. Old Key Lime House, Lantana
D2 300 E Ocean Ave
Sublime key lime pie and seafood in a house dating from 1889.

9. Joanie's Blue Crab Café, Ochopee
An Everglades pit stop *(p136)* serving delicacies such as frogs' legs, gator pieces, and Indian fry bread.

10. Robert Is Here, Homestead
This celebrated fruit stand *(p119)* always draws a crowd for its smoothies and key lime milkshakes.

OFF THE BEATEN PATH

House on stilts over the sea, Stiltsville

1 Stiltsville, Key Biscayne

H4 stiltsvilletrust.org

Drive to the southernmost tip of Key Biscayne, look way out over the water, and you'll spy seven fragile-looking structures built on stilts. These fishers' bungalows are the last of what was once a much larger community from the 1930s to 1960s. Their number has dwindled due to hurricanes, and the site is now overseen by the Stiltsville Trust (public access is by permit only).

2 The Kampong

One of Miami's lesser-visited gems, this tropical garden *(p108)* is sited southwest of downtown Coconut Grove. The former estate of horticulturalist David Fairchild, it holds an impressive collection of tropical flowers, fruit trees, and plants.

3 Los Pinareños Fruteria

This fruit stand and outdoor café *(p98)* in the heart of Little Havana seems transported straight from Cuba. Afro-Cuban tunes waft through boxes of papaya, oranges, guavas, and coconuts, while plates of chicken rice and fresh juices are doled out from the kitchen.

4 Overtown

G3 Lyric Theater: 819 NW 2nd Ave bahlt.org

Miami's African American community thrived in this segregated neighborhood after the incorporation of the city in 1896. Remnants of the area's glory days include the beautifully renovated Lyric Theater, opened in 1913. It acts as a cultural center today, home to the Black Archives museum.

5 Ermita de la Caridad Church, Coconut Grove

M5 3609 S Miami Ave, Coconut Grove 305 854 2404 7am–9pm Mon–Sat, 7am–7pm Sun

Built in the late 1960s, this peculiar conical church is the religious heart

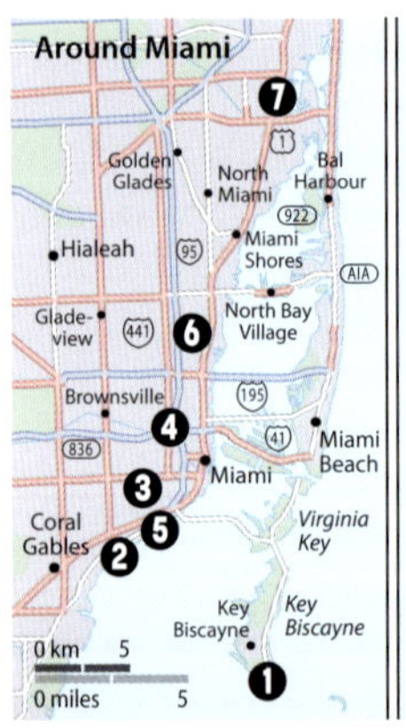

Palm trees surrounding Ermita de la Caridad Church

of expat Cuban life. Beneath the altar there's a cache of Cuban soil and sand, salvaged from a refugee boat, while above it a mural depicts the history of the Catholic Church in Cuba. The shrine is dedicated to Our Lady of Charity, the Cuban patron saint (the statue inside is a replica of the revered original from the shrine in El Cobre).

6 Santería and Vodou Botánicas

For an insight into the practice of the hybrid Caribbean religions of Santería and Vodou (or Voodoo) – West African ritual and belief blended with Roman Catholicism – visit the *botánicas* (traditional folk medicine shops) in Little Haiti (p101). These stores carry all sorts of potions, candles, statuary, and glass jars packed with herbs.

7 Ancient Spanish Monastery

Built in 1133 near Segovia, this medieval monastery *(p101)* was occupied by Cistercian monks for almost 700 years. In 1925, publisher William Randolph Hearst acquired the building and had it shipped to the US in more than 11,000 crates. However, the stones languished in a warehouse in New York until 1952, when the decision was finally made to reconstruct the monastery on US soil. Today, it functions as a working church, serving a growing congregation and attracting many visitors.

8 Nancy Forrester's Secret Garden, Key West

Local artist Nancy Forrester and her friends began working on this lush, funky, and indefinable Key West garden *(p53)* in the 1970s.

9 No Name Pub

B6 30813 Watson Blvd, Big Pine Key nonamepub.com

This no-frills bar and restaurant started as a 1930s general store, before the pub was added in 1936.

10 The "Garden of Eden," Key West

A6 The Bull and Whistle Bar, 3/F, 224 Duval St, Key West Noon–3am daily bullkeywest.org

Devoted nudists can find an appreciative milieu in this renowned bar set inside the Bull and Whistle Bar *(p130)*, as well as within the walls and gardens of many guesthouses scattered around town.

Popular Garden of Eden on Duval Street

FAMILY ATTRACTIONS

The Key West Butterfly and Nature Conservatory

1 The Key West Butterfly and Nature Conservatory

A6 1316 Duval St, Key West 9am–5pm daily keywestbutterfly.com

Take a magical stroll through the conservatory filled with hundreds of beautiful butterflies, flowering plants, trees, birds, and cascading waterfalls in this climate-controlled, glass-enclosed habitat.

2 Pinecrest Gardens

F4 11000 Red Rd, Pinecrest 9am–5pm daily pinecrestgardens.org

There's plenty for kids to enjoy here: a Splash N Play area, mangrove forest, colorful playground, domino games, and a giant chess and checkers board, along with children's theater performances, concerts, and movies.

3 Miami Children's Museum

G3 980 MacArthur Causeway 10am–6pm daily miamichildrensmuseum.org

Play, learn, imagine, and create at this museum. Interactive exhibits related to the arts, culture, and communication are on offer. Catch a fish in the waterfall or take a trip on a pretend cruise ship complete with portholes.

4 Amelia Earhart Park

G2 401 E 65th St, Hialeah 305 685 8389 Sunrise–sunset daily

Come to this park for a fun and wholesome family day out. There's a watersports complex with wake-surfing and waterskiing, bike rentals, hiking and mountain biking trails, volleyball courts, and soccer fields. There are playgrounds and fish-filled lakes as well. The whole park is delightfully uncrowded, as it is well away from the tourist track.

5 Phillip and Patricia Frost Museum of Science

G3 1101 Biscayne Blvd 10am–6pm daily frostscience.org

The young and curious will find much to capture their attention and imagination here. There are over 140 hands-on exhibits to explore the worlds of sound, light, and gravity. Head to the "MeLab", which focuses on health and wellbeing, or "Crush the Calories" a digital gaming installation. Outside – beyond the collections of fossils, mounted insects, spiders, and butterflies – lies the Wildlife Center,

Enjoying MeLab at the Phillip and Patricia Frost Museum of Science

home to birds, tortoises, and enormous snakes. The planetarium offers laser light shows set to rock music.

6 Turtle Hospital

B6 2396 Overseas Hwy, Marathon 9am–4pm daily turtlehospital.org

Based on Key Vaca, the Turtle Hospital is a rescue, rehabilitation, and release facility for injured turtles recovered from all over the Keys. Since its opening in 1986, it has successfully treated and released more than 2,000 turtles. There are guided tours of the hospital and rehabilitation sections where you can meet some of the current patients too, which is a great highlight for kids. It also houses several permanent residents deemed unreleasable by the Florida Wildlife Commission.

7 HistoryMiami Museum

The Downtown museum *(p48)* has a number of hands-on activities and multimedia programs, such as an exploration of the past and present ecology of the Everglades.

8 Cape Florida Light

Older kids love clambering up this 95-ft- (30-m-) high lighthouse (children under-8 are not permitted to go up), while the surrounding beaches of Bill Baggs Cape Florida State Park *(p84)* are entertaining for the whole family.

9 Hobie Island Beach

An excellent stretch of beach *(p55)*, popular with windsurfers and also with families appreciative of its calm, shallow waters.

10 Boat Tours, Biscayne Bay

P1 Island Queen Cruises, 401 Biscayne Blvd, Bayside Marketplace 11am–6pm Mon–Fri, 11am–7pm Sat & Sun islandqueencruises.com

Narrated boat tours are the best way to see the islands of Biscayne Bay – the tranquil stretch of water between Downtown and Miami Beach – which is dominated by opulent mansions owned by celebrities such as Shaquille O'Neal and Oprah Winfrey.

Boat sightseeing tour of Biscayne Bay

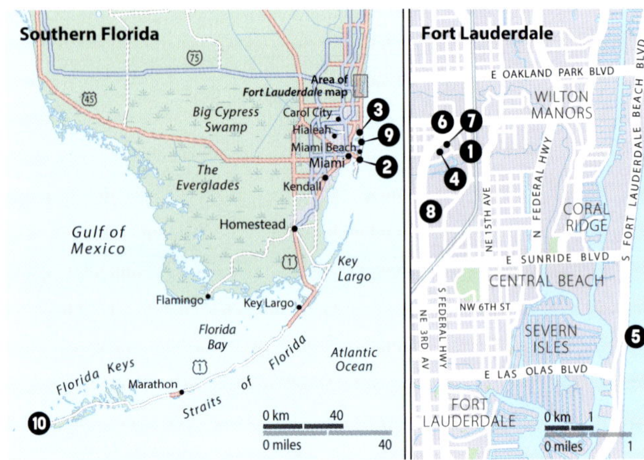

LGBTQ+ VENUES

1 Pride Center at Equality Park

D3 2040 N Dixie Hwy, Wilton Manors 954 463 9005

Located a few miles north of Fort Lauderdale, in the town of Wilton Manors (one of South Florida's biggest LGBTQ+ towns), this is a well-maintained center. There's an extensive library of LGBTQ+ literature and reference works, friendly and helpful staff, a full calendar of special events, and plenty of opportunities for lively social interaction.

Strolling a vibrant street in Wilton Manors

2 Beach at 12th Street, SoBe

S3–S4

This beautiful sandy stretch of SoBe, with its rainbow flags flying, is one of the most popular beaches among the LGBTQ+ community.

3 Haulover Park Beach, Miami Beach

H1

Everyone is welcome at this pristine stretch of shoreline. The northern portion is a designated nude area where clothing is very much optional.

4 Shoppes of Wilton Manors, Broward County

D3 2262 Wilton Dr

The "gayborhood" of Wilton Manors is home to LGBTQ+-friendly businesses, the Stonewall National Museum and Archives, and the annual Stonewall Pride Festival.

5 Fort Lauderdale LGBTQ+ Beaches

D3

Two major beaches in the Fort Lauderdale area are LGBTQ+ friendly,

Sunseekers at the popular Fort Lauderdale Beach

and particularly popular with gay men: Sebastian Street Beach; and Dr. Von D. Mizell-Eula Johnson State Park.

6 Pub on the Drive

D3 2283 Wilton Dr, Wilton Manors 9am–2am daily thepubwm.com

This is another Wilton Manors mainstay, beloved for its open-air patio, all-day two-for-one "happy hour," and dancing until 2am. Drag shows take place several nights a week and fun karaoke and trivia nights are hosted on Wednesdays. There are other events and variety shows every night.

7 Georgie's Alibi Monkey Bar

D3 2266 Wilton Dr, Wilton Manors alibiwiltonmanors.com

This restaurant, sports bar, and video bar opened in 1997 in what was a rundown area, but Wilton Manors has since blossomed and this bar has flourished with it. The Alibi is one of South Florida's best LGBTQ+ venues, serving American classics, with affordable nightly drink specials.

8 Ramrod, Fort Lauderdale

D3 1508 NE 4th Ave 954 763 8219

Fort Lauderdale's Ramrod is a leather and uniform bar with a welcoming crowd. The place is packed on Friday and Saturday nights. There's usually a line at the door, but it's worth the wait. Fantastic DJs make this a great party scene, and on some Saturdays they host intro nights to queer leather and kink.

9 LGBT+ Visitor Center

R3 1130 Washington Ave, South Beach 305 397 8914

Set in the Old City Hall, Miami's LGBT+ center offers information, publications, and free Wi-Fi. It hosts great events, and also helps with last-minute hotel bookings, tours, dinner reservations, and recommendations.

10 Key West Business Guild

A6

Established in 1978, this LGBTQ+ organization operates the Gay Key West Visitor Center *(gaykeywestfl.com)* at 808 Duval Street. It has information about the island, local businesses and events such as Tropical Heat, Key West Pride, Key West Womenfest, and the Headdress Ball.

Pride flags on Duval Street, Key West

PERFORMING ARTS VENUES

Entrance to the Art Deco-style Colony Theatre

1 Colony Theatre

Q2 1040 Lincoln Rd, Miami Beach miaminewdrama.org

Enjoy the city's best music, dance, comedy, and theater performances here. It's also home to Miami New Drama, a non-profit theater company.

2 Miami-Dade County Auditorium

G3 2901 W Flagler St miamidadecountyauditorium.org

Built in 1951, this venue is proud to have been one of the first in the country to host the late Luciano Pavarotti, when he was still a virtual unknown. Operas, concerts, and events all benefit from the excellent acoustics in the auditorium.

3 Miracle Theatre

G3 280 Miracle Mile, Coral Gables actorsplayhouse.org

The 1940s Deco-style movie theater was converted into a playhouse in 1995 and has won accolades for musicals such as *West Side Story*.

4 Olympia Theater

Opened in 1926, the historic Olympia Theater *(p97)*, located in Downtown Miami, is a major venue offering a varied program of plays, music, dance, and film.

5 Adrienne Arsht Center for the Performing Arts

G3 1300 Biscayne Blvd arshtcenter.org

This spectacular complex includes three state-of-the-art theaters, the Ziff Ballet Opera House, Knight Concert Hall, and a restored Art Deco tower.

6 Broward Center

D3 201 SW 5th Ave, Fort Lauderdale browardcenter.org

This arts center opened in 1991 at the heart of the Riverwalk Arts and Entertainment District. Key partners include the Symphony of the Americas, Florida Grand Opera, and Miami City Ballet.

7 Wertheim Performing Arts Center

F3 10910 SW 17th St carta.fiu.edu/the-wertheim

West of Downtown on the campus of Florida International University, this state-of-the-art venue comprises the

Tedeschi Trucks performing at the Kravis Center

Mainstage Theatre, the Concert Hall, and the Black Box Studio Theatre. It is also home to the FIU School of Music and Department of Theatre.

8 The Fillmore Miami Beach at the Jackie Gleason Theater

R2 1700 Washington Ave, Miami Beach fillmoremb.com

A premiere Art Deco concert venue, the Jackie Gleason Theater is famed for hosting a variety of performances.

9 New World Center

R2 500 17th St, Miami Beach nws.edu

Home to the New World Symphony, which trains and prepares music graduates, this institution showcases young virtuosos performing everything from gospel and Piazzolla tango to symphonies and chamber works.

10 Kravis Center

D2 701 Okeechobee Blvd, W Palm Beach kravis.org

This performing arts center houses the Palm Beach Opera and Palm Beach Pops. It also has a concert hall, the Rinker Playhouse, the Helen K. Persson Hall and the Cohen Pavilion ballroom and events hall.

TOP 10 ENTERTAINERS IN MIAMI

Singer Cher in concert

1. Cher
You can see where the iconic singer lived with Sonny on the water in Fort Lauderdale and South Beach.

2. Don Johnson
The star of *Miami Vice* *(p84)*, this King of 1980s Cool helped put hip "new" South Beach on the map.

3. Jackie Gleason
"The Great One" brought his *Jackie Gleason Show* permanently to Miami in 1964.

4. Madonna
"The Queen of Pop" once owned a piece of the former Delano Hotel.

5. Dave Barry
The newspaper humorist and author has helped to create Miami's image as an over-the-top urban free-for-all.

6. Gloria Estefan
This pop songstress has succeeded in building an impressive cultural and real-estate empire.

7. Rosie O'Donnell
The talkshow hostess calls West Palm Beach home and is involved in local politics.

8. Jennifer Lopez
This Latin American actress and songstress has owned a mansion and estate at Miami Beach since 2002.

9. Flo Rida
The rapper grew up in Greater Miami and still lives in the area.

10. Tito Puente, Jr.
This talented musician has made South Florida home, where he promotes LGBTQ+ causes.

NIGHTS OUT

1 Watr at the Rooftop

Atop the trendy 1 Hotel, Watr *(p89)* is decked out in reclaimed wood and draws a trendy crowd with its relaxed, breezy vibe, and expansive 18th-floor views across South Beach. There's also a menu of Peruvian-Japanese snacks.

2 Twist

SoBe's premier LGBTQ+ venue *(p88)* is a hugely popular hotspot that comes alive late at night. Open until dawn, this sprawling space features seven distinct bars, each offering its own unique music, decor, and vibe.

3 Salsa Mia

S4 900 Ocean Dr
salsamia.com

If you want an active outing, try the two-hour salsa class and learn to sway to the sizzling sound of a live band performing Miami's signature music. Dance lessons and party packages are available until 5 in the morning.

4 Mynt

Enjoy a menu of custom cocktails at this vibrant, hot nightspot *(p89)* in South Beach. The lively crowd here, including the celebrity elite, enjoy partying in style to house and hip-hop, although there is no real dance floor.

5 Escape Lounge

D3 300 SW 1st Ave, Fort Lauderdale 11pm–4am Fri–Sun
escapelounge.club

This glamorous club and lounge bar is a popular choice in Fort Lauderdale. It is known for its tempting drink deals on Fridays and its free Latin nights on Saturdays.

6 El Patio

G3 167 NW 23rd St
elpatiowynwood.com

This south-of-the-border-style venue plays throbbing reggae and Latin music, and offers deals during happy hours. There are excellent live performances, too.

7 E11EVEN Miami

G3 29 NE 11th St
11miami.com

Located in Downtown Miami's entertainment district, E11EVEN Miami is a part cabaret and part nightclub. A Florida institution, it

Live performance in full swing at E11EVEN

features trapeze artists, a rooftop lounge, and a roster of in-house performers and top DJs. The rooftop restaurant offers a variety of late-night munchies.

8 Nikki Beach Miami Beach

This beachfront complex is a playground for the hip and trendy denizens of SoBe. Nikki Beach *(p89)* is located on the first floor and Club 01 is on the second. There are new themes and dances every week, fashion shows, and interactive entertainment.

9 Basement

Rub shoulders with Hollywood glitterati at one of Miami's hottest micro-clubs *(p89)*. This hip party spot has a strobe-lit dance floor, a bowling alley, and a mini ice-skating rink, all of which add to its retro, Studio 54 vibe.

10 Bodega Taqueria y Tequila

This Miami Beach club *(p89)* offers a lively atmosphere and an impressive selection of drinks, including signature margaritas and tequila-based cocktails. With its lineup of weekend events, live music, DJs, happy hours, and screens showing big sport games, it's a go-to spot for locals and visitors alike in South Beach.

Enjoying the nightclub vibe at Mynt

TOP 10 TROPICAL TIPPLES

1. Mojito
An all-time classic, this cocktail blends light rum with crushed mint leaves, sugar, and lime to taste.

2. Hurricane
Mix dark and light rums, blue Curaçao, and lemon juice, and enjoy.

3. Piña Colada
The blend of coconut milk, pineapple juice, and rum is impossible to beat.

4. Rum Runner
Shades of Prohibition-era Caribbean smugglers, this classic comes in many styles and fruity flavors: watermelon, grenadine, blackberry, etc.

5. Sangria
The variations of fruit added to the red wine are almost endless.

6. Cosmopolitan
Variations on this vodka and Cointreau theme are creative. Often done with cranberry and/or orange notes.

7. Martini
Be prepared for this old standby to appear on the menu in a thousand creative guises: with unexpected fruit liqueurs, for example, or even blended with white or milk chocolate.

8. Margarita
This south-of-the-border treat, in regular and frozen incarnations, may be paired with any fruit and a range of liqueurs, too.

9. Mai Tai
One version of this Polynesian perennial features *crème de noyaux*, banana, grenadine, and tropical juices.

10. Daiquiri
Hemingway's favorite cocktail is a timeless Caribbean rum concoction, prepared with flavors like mango, strawberry, lime, and peach.

Refreshing glass of daiquiri

LOCAL DISHES

1 Blackened Grouper

Having your fish cooked blackened is a Cajun recipe that has caught on in most restaurants in South Florida. The blackening technique was pioneered by local chef Paul Prudhomme in the 1980s, and involves using a special mix of spices before charring the fish over a hot cast-iron skillet. There are various species of grouper in the waters around Florida, and its mild flavor perfectly complements the hit of spice.

2 Conch Chowder

The conch, a snail- or slug-like mollusk that lives in beautiful pink shells, is served up in a traditional, rather chewy dish across the Caribbean, and Floridians have perfected their own version of this wonderfully flavorsome chowder. You can also try conch fried as delightfully crispy fritters.

3 Black Beans and Rice

"Moros y Cristianos" is a staple of the Cuban diet, and with good reason. Every forkful contains a symphony of smoky Latin flavors, with hints of cumin, oregano, and garlic. The smokiness of the dish complements almost everything, and you'll find steaming bowls of the stuff served alongside meat or fish in popular Cuban eateries across Little Havana.

A street-food vendor serving black beans and rice

Grilled beef steak with chimichurri sauce

4 Chimichurri

As delicious as it is versatile, this sauce is made of olive oil, garlic, lemon juice or wine vinegar, parsley, and jalapeño peppers (for those who like it hot). You're as likely to find chimichurri basted over roasted meats as you are served as a dipping sauce for freshly baked Cuban bread.

5 Yucca

Yucca (the edible root of cassava) and plantain (a starchy fruit related to the banana) are often deep-fried and served together in Cuban cuisine. They take on a chip-like shape and texture, with each bite slightly sweet and wonderfully aromatic. The chips are a perfect street food or a good accompaniment to a meaty main.

6 Ceviche

This seafood classic is raw fish marinaded in lime juice, onions, green bell peppers, and cilantro (coriander), and is best enjoyed with the freshest fish. It's typically eaten cold, all the better to appreciate its delicate citrus flavor. You'll find it served in Miami's many ocean-facing bars and diners.

7 Lechon Asado

Pork is an integral source of protein in the Cuban diet. *Lechon asado* translates as "roast suckling pig", and this hearty dish is served as a decadent centerpiece in many of Miami's Latin restaurants. Recipes vary, but the meat is usually marinaded in *mojo*, a delectably sweet and spicy sauce made from oranges, oregano, and garlic.

8 Mofongo

Puerto Rican food is everywhere in Miami, and *mofongo* is a firm favorite. Again, it celebrates the humble plantain, with the fruit picked before fully ripened, fried, and then mashed into a tight ball with salt, garlic and pork.

9 Alfajores

Recipes vary from country to country, but these delightful shortbread-like pastries are popular across Latin America. In Miami, they are typically composed of chocolate, custard, and coconut. They can be bought pre-made in packets, but they are best enjoyed freshly baked from a bakery like Delizzia *(4259 West Flagler Street)*.

10 Key Lime Pie

Key limes, small citrus fruits that look more like lemons, make the most exquisite pie. This is the definitive Florida dessert, marrying the tang of lime juice with a pillowy meringue or indulgent whipped cream topping.

A fine slice of Key lime pie

TOP 10 FOOD-CART STAPLES

Baja fish tacos

1. Grilled Cheese
A favorite at Miami's many food carts, these toasties are served hot with a variety of additional fillings.

2. Tacos
Miami has pushed the boat out with its reinventions of the taco: look out for tofu, fish, or sweet varieties.

3. Bubble Tea
Those on the west coast might call it boba, but here this ubiquitous Asian favorite is known as bubble tea.

4. Empanadas
You'll find every variety of empanada at Miami's food trucks.

5. Fried Chicken
Chicken in a beer eel reduction? Sounds odd, but Miami's food trucks have transformed humble poultry.

6. Popsicles
The Miami popsicle marries the nostalgic iced treat with a host of artisanal flavors.

7. Café Cubano (Cafecito)
A tiny cup of sweet, black coffee is the mainstay of life for many. Act like a local, and get it from a coffee truck.

8. Fritas
A *frita* is a Cuban street-food staple: a decadent pork burger loaded with shoestring fries, onion, and ketchup.

9. Matcha Treats
Matcha is now everywhere in Miami: you'll find matcha frappés, matcha cookies, and matcha macarons.

10. Arepa
These stuffable Venezuelan flatbreads come loaded with delectable fillings.

SHOPPING CENTERS

1 Bal Harbour Shops

H2 9700 Collins Ave 11am–10pm Mon–Sat, noon–6pm Sun balharbourshops.com

The ultimate in chi-chi, down to the English spelling of "Harbour", this is one of Miami's first high-fashion malls. It opened in 1965, and is now home to the likes of Burberry, Versace, Tiffany, and Prada, along with several fine dining options, all surrounded by tropical gardens.

2 Dadeland Mall

F4 7535 N Kendall Dr simon.com/mall/dadeland-mall

Fear not – there is a Saks Fifth Avenue even way down in South Miami – plus some 170 high-end specialty stores and several other fine anchor stores, including the state's largest Macy's. The decor is pleasing, if a bit predictable, with palm-tree pillars and ceilings painted to resemble the sky.

3 Collins Avenue from 6th to 9th Street, SoBe

This area *(p87)* is great to stroll and shop. There are boutique hotels, cigar shops, and cafés interspersed with lower-priced stores such as Shoe Palace and Armani Exchange. A variety of price ranges makes this area one for the whole family to shop in.

4 Aventura Mall

H1 19501 Biscayne Blvd aventuramall.com

Department stores Bloomingdale's and Nordstrom are the upscale anchors at this mall, spread over three levels. Specialty stores include Hugo Boss, Anthropologie, and Michael Kors. Art installations, excellent restaurants, and a cineplex complete the picture.

5 Shops at Merrick Park

G3 358 San Lorenzo Ave, Coral Gables shopsatmerrickpark.com

The Shops at Merrick Park offers luxury retail stores amid a posh urban garden. At its heart are Neiman Marcus and Miami's first Nordstrom, along with restaurants, such as the elegant Perry's Steakhouse.

6 Las Olas Boulevard and the Galleria

D3 2414 E Sunrise Blvd, Fort Lauderdale galleriamall-fl.com

Las Olas's 100-plus boutiques are unique, and are interspersed with some really good restaurants.

7 The Falls

F4 8888 SW 136th St simon.com/mall/the-falls

Semi-open-air arcades with waterfalls and tropical vegetation form the back-

Miami's upscale Bal Harbour Shops

drop to over 100 shops. The stores here include Macy's, Coach, Sephora, and the Adventure Kids amusement area.

8 Town Center at Boca Raton

D3 Town Center 6000 W Glades Rd simon.com/mall/town-center-at-boca-raton

Set amid tropical foliage, skylights, and sculptural accents, Boca's premiere mall offers luxury and a fancy cuisine court.

9 Duval Street, Key West

A6

Key West's main thoroughfare, Duval Street is lined with souvenir shops and often bustling with tourists. It is home to superb emporiums of quality merchandise, including clothing at Stitches of Key West (No. 533) and shoes at Birkenstock (No. 610).

10 Worth Avenue, Palm Beach

Worth Avenue offers the quintessential Palm Beach luxury shopping experience, with a range of stores and fine boutiques. The avenue features expensive, ultra-exclusive must-haves for the rich and famous.

Lilly Pulitzer store on Worth Avenue, Palm Beach

TOP 10 MALLS AND MARKET

1. Sawgrass Mills Mall
D3 12801 W Sunrise Blvd, Flamingo Rd
This 8-acre (3-ha) mall comprises more than 350 discount outlets, from high-fashion brands to value retailers.

2. Bayside Marketplace
Chain boutiques abound in this sprawling marketplace *(p94)*.

3. Lincoln Road Markets
R2 Lincoln Rd, between Washington Ave & Alton Rd
A lively pedestrian area offering markets such as Lincoln Road Farmers' Market, which sells regional products.

4. 1-800-Lucky
G2 143 NW 23rd St, Wynwood
The first food hall in Miami devoted to Asian cuisine, it serves everything from ramen to Peking duck.

5. Los Pinareños Fruteria
Little Havana's foremost fruit and vegetable market *(p98)*.

6. The Swap Shop
D3 3291 W Sunrise Blvd, Fort Lauderdale
This huge flea market features antiques, collectibles, clothing, plants, and a farmers' market.

7. Dania Beach Historic Antiques District
D3 Federal Hwy 1 north for two blocks from Dania Beach Blvd
With an array of furniture, fine art, and jewelry, this is South Florida's largest concentration of antiques shops.

8. Opa-Locka Flea Market
G2 13449 NW 42nd Ave
Around 200 vendors occupy the air-conditioned indoor space selling accessories, clothing, decor, and more.

9. Española Way Market
R3 15th St, South Beach
On Sundays, there's a small market selling flowers and organic products.

10. Dolphin Mall
F3 11401 NW 12th St
More than 200 stores are crammed into one of Greater Miami's most popular middle-range malls.

MIAMI AND THE KEYS FOR FREE

1 A Day on South Beach

With so much happening on land, it's easy to overlook Miami's biggest free attraction: the beach itself *(p22)*. South Beach is home to sandy strands, swaying palms, the pastel-colored Art Deco buildings, and those famous candy-colored lifeguard towers that have become synonymous with this iconic destination.

2 Stroll Along Lincoln Road Mall

Pedestrianized Lincoln Road Mall *(p84)* is an upscale shopping strip lined with fashionable brand-name stores, restaurants, bars, al-fresco cafés, and art galleries, making it a must-see for anyone visiting the city. Sunday afternoons here are especially lively.

Walking along the Lincoln Road Mall on South Beach

3 Holocaust Memorial

Miami's moving tribute to the Holocaust depicts a giant bronze arm tattooed with an Auschwitz number reaching toward the sky. The black marble walls around the sculpture *(p47)* are inscribed with the names of the victims of Nazi atrocities.

4 Miami Circle

N2 · Brickell Ave, Downtown

Just across the Brickell Avenue Bridge south of Downtown Miami, a small park preserves the ring of 24 holes known as the Miami Circle. The site was discovered by accident in 1998, and the prehistoric shell-tools found here were used to carbon-date the site to between 1,700 and 2,000 years old.

5 Mallory Square Sunset Celebration, Key West

A6 · Mallory Square Dock, Key West · sunsetcelebration.org

Key West's Sunset Celebration started in the 1960s. Today, these nightly gatherings, starting at sunset, feature arts and crafts, jugglers, fire-eaters, food carts, and cheap cocktails as a backdrop for the sinking of the sun.

6 Cubaocho Museum

This dynamic Cuban American cultural center *(p94)* hosts exhibits of Cuban art and a roster of live events. Visitors can also relax at a traditional café and a bar serving amazing mojitos.

7 Tour the Wynwood Walls

G3 · 2520 NW 2nd Ave, between NW 25th and NW 26th Sts · 11am–7pm daily (to 8pm Fri & Sat) · thewynwoodwalls.com

The Wynwood district is a magnet for art enthusiasts, with a vibrant and ever-evolving street-art scene that

Vibrant mural at Miami's iconic Wynwood Walls

has transformed the area into a global art destination. Packed with galleries and adorned with giant murals known as the Wynwood Walls, the area's main creative hub thrives along 2nd Avenue, just north of Downtown Miami. Keep an eye out for hidden gems tucked away in corners and down alleyways.

8 Institute of Contemporary Art, Miami

G2 61 NE 41st St 11am–6pm Wed–Sun icamiami.org

The city's top contemporary art museum, the Institute of Contemporary Art, Miami (ICA Miami) focuses on local, emerging, and under-recognized artists, while also promoting continuous experimentation in contemporary art.

9 Florida Keys Eco-Discovery Center

A6 35 Quay Rd, Key West 9am–4pm Wed–Sat floridakeys.noaa.gov/eco_discovery.html

This center offers visitors and locals the opportunity to explore the region's remarkable ecology.

10 Observing Key Deer on Big Pine Key

B6 10am–3pm Wed–Sat fws.gov/nationalkeydeer

Big Pine Key is known for its herds of feral Key deer. The best time to spot them is at sunrise or sunset.

TOP 10 BUDGET TIPS

1. Free yoga
Free yoga classes are held on Thursday at Bayfront Park and on Lincoln Rd.

2. Monthly art walks
Visit Coral Gables and Wynwood when the free monthly art walks/gallery nights take place.

3. Free museums
Try to visit museums on free days, such as the Jewish Museum (Saturday) and The Wolfsonian-FIU (Friday nights).

4. Go Miami pass
Buy a Go Miami pass *(gocity.com/miami)* to enjoy exclusive discounts of up to 55 per cent at around 25 major attractions.

5. Travel during off-peak season
To save money avoid traveling during the peak season. January to April is the most expensive time.

6. Take the bus
On arrival in Miami, save by taking the Miami Beach Airport Express bus rather than a taxi.

7. Rent a bike
Not only is cycling healthier than driving, but it's also one of the best ways to see the sights.

8. Dine early
Seek out dinner deals such as early-bird specials for patrons dining between 5pm and 6pm.

9. Try street food
Little Havana's Latin American and Cuban restaurants are much less expensive than South Beach.

10. Go to the beach
Beaches are free and open to the public, even if parking is not.

Lifeguard tower, Miami Beach

FESTIVALS AND EVENTS

1 South Beach Wine and Food Festival

Feb **W** sobewff.org

This popular festival celebrates the talents of renowned wine producers and local and guest chefs.

2 Coconut Grove Arts Festival

3rd weekend in Feb

The Grove is one of the biggest arts festivals *(p111)* in the country, complete with all-day concerts, street food, and throngs of arts lovers.

3 Winter Party

Late Feb–early Mar

W winterparty.com

This renowned annual LGBTQ+ beach party attracts thousands of visitors from all over the United States.

Enjoying a band performance during Carnaval Miami

4 Carnaval Miami

Early Mar **W** carnavalmiami.com

For the Cuban district, March is a time of dancing and singing in the streets to Latin jazz, pop, flamenco, and tango. It culminates on the second Sunday with a large party. Twenty-three blocks of Little Havana are closed off and performers line the way. A fireworks display brings a resounding finale to the festivities.

5 Miami-Dade County Fair and Exposition

Mar/Apr **W** thefair.me

This traditional American county fair is replete with rides, sideshows, cotton candy, candied apples, live performances, and exhibits relating to farm life and crafts.

6 Miami Film Festival

Early Apr **W** miamifilm festival.com

Organized by the Film Society of Miami and Miami Dade College (MDC), the Miami Film Festival especially focuses on Ibero-American films. Venues for the event include the Silverspot Cinema in Downtown Miami, Coral Gables Art Cinema, and the Bill Cosford Cinema.

7 International Mango Festival

Mid-Jul

Held annually at the Fairchild Tropical Botanic Garden, this festival celebrates

Miami Film Festival at Miami Dade College

the mango with a wide variety of the fruit and a full feast dedicated to it. Enjoy tastings and an array of mango-inspired dishes, desserts, and drinks.

8 Hispanic Heritage Festival

Sep/Oct

This month-long Latin American celebration has street parties, food festivals, films, music and dance performances, and a fashion show.

9 Fantasy Fest

Mid–late Oct

For two weeks leading up to Halloween, Key West gives itself over to nonstop celebration *(p127)*. On the Saturday before the 31st, a parade, featuring floats and costumes, departs from Mallory Square and slowly winds its way down Duval Street. Thousands of revelers, including island-style dancers in elaborate costumes, attend this adults-only parade.

10 King Mango Strut

Late Dec–early Jan

A Coconut Grove spoof on the Orange Bowl Parade *(p111)*, this annual parade features satirical costumes, colorful floats, and marching bands.

Costumed revelers at the Fantasy Fest, Key West

TOP 10 MUSIC EVENTS AND FESTIVALS

1. Mile 0 Festival
Late Jan–Feb W mile0fest.com
The best Red Dirt and Americana musicians come to Key West.

2. Festival of the Arts Boca
Mar W festivalboca.org
This festival showcases globally acclaimed classical music ranging from traditional symphonies to contemporary compositions.

3. Jazz in the Gardens
Mar W jazzinthegardens.com
Internationally renowned jazz and R&B performances at the Hard Rock Stadium.

4. Winter Music Conference
Mar W wintermusicconference.com
A week-long electronic music conference, held on Miami Beach.

5. Rolling Loud Miami
Mid–Mar W rollingloud.com/miami
Begun in Miami, this three-day event is the world's largest hip-hop festival.

6. Ultra Music Festival
Late Mar W ultramusicfestival.com
The world's premier electronic music festival takes place in Bayfront Park.

7. Tortuga Music Festival
Apr W tortugamusicfestival.com
This country, rock, and roots festival funds marine conservation.

8. Afro Roots Festival
Late Apr–May
Live concerts and events celebrating Pan-African music take place across the Keys.

9. Lower Keys Underwater Music Festival
Jul
Unique sub-sea concert held at Looe Key Reef Resort & Dive Center.

10. Ill Points
Oct W iiipoints.com
The Mana Wynwood Convention Center hosts a music, art, and technology festival.

AREA BY AREA

Art Deco hotels on Ocean Drive

STARLITE
STARLITE HOTEL
HOTEL

MIAMI BEACH AND KEY BISCAYNE

With its stunning shoreline and pastel-colored Art Deco buildings along Ocean Drive, Miami Beach attracts visitors to its world-class beaches, shopping, food, and thrilling nightlife. South Beach (or SoBe) is particularly famous for its retro look, alluring sands, and high-end fashion boutiques. An array of museums and annual art festivals add to the cultural life of the neighborhood. Farther afield, Key Biscayne, the next big island to the south, provides a contrast to the dynamism of its neighbor; here you will find a tranquil and family-oriented atmosphere pervading parks and perfect beaches.

For places to stay in this area, see p148

1 SoBe and the Art Deco District

All walks of life meet here in the vibrant community of South Beach, otherwise known as SoBe *(p22)*. Its famous Art Deco District *(p24)* is beautifully preserved in hundreds of colorful, Tropical Deco buildings.

2 The Bass

S1 2100 Collins Ave, South Beach Noon–5pm Wed–Sun (6–9pm third Thu of the month) thebass.org

This Mayan-influenced Art Deco structure of the 1930s, previously the Miami Beach Public Library and Art Center, came of age in 1964, when John and Johanna Bass donated their extensive collection of art. It consists mainly of 15th- to 17th-century European paintings, sculpture, and textiles; highlights include Renaissance and Baroque works, as well as paintings by Rubens, and a 16th-century Flemish tapestry.

Miami Beach

1 mile (1.6 km) 9 2

See map left

Venetian Islands

VENETIAN WAY

MACARTHUR CAUSEWAY

Lummus Island

Fisher Island

Biscayne Bay

10 6 2 3 8 1

RICKENBACKER CAUSEWAY

Virginia Key

Atlantic Ocean

8

7

CRANDON BOULEVARD

Key Biscayne

Biscayne Bay

Key Biscayne

5

6

0 km 1

0 miles 1

3 Flamingo Park

R3 11th St and Jefferson Ave, South Beach 305 673 7779 Sunrise–sunset daily

This pleasant spot in the heart of South Beach started life in the 1920s as a golf course. Later home to major and minor league baseball teams, the 36-acre- (14-ha-) park has since been extensively renovated. Its walking trails are now surrounded by lush landscaping, and today the site hosts an array of sports facilities, including baseball and football stadiums, basketball, handball, and tennis courts, and a soccer field. There is also a state-of-the-art aquatic center with two public pools, a playground for toddlers, and a "bark park", complete with amenities for your canine friends.

Flamingos relaxing by the water in Flamingo Park

4 Lincoln Road Mall

R2

Acclaimed as the most glamorous shopping district outside of New York when it debuted in the 1950s, this pedestrianized strip remains lined with hip brand-name stores and cool cafés. Russian-born "Miami Modern" (MiMo) architect Morris Lapidus designed the mall, including its gardens and space-age follies that serve as sunshades. Attractions include Oolite Arts (at No. 924), where avant-garde artwork is displayed.

5 Bill Baggs Cape Florida State Park

H4 8am–sunset daily floridastateparks.org

This beach is conveniently joined to picnic areas and pavilions by boardwalks across the dunes. The sugary sand is sometimes marred by clumps of seaweed, but it is the stinging Portuguese man-o'-war that you need to look out for.

6 Cape Florida Lighthouse

H4 Tours at 10am & 1pm Thu–Mon

Set near the tip of Bill Baggs Cape Florida State Park, this historic lighthouse is the oldest structure in South Florida, standing sentinel since 1825. In 1836, it was destroyed by Indigenous peoples, only to be reconstructed ten years later. It has since withstood meteorological onslaughts, and in 1966 its renovation and preservation began.

7 Crandon Park

H4 305 365 2320

Key Biscayne is blessed with some of Miami's top beaches. On the upper half of the key, Crandon is 3 miles (5 km) long and very wide, with palm trees and picnic areas. Its waters are calm and shallow, and good for snorkeling.

8 Marjory Stoneman Douglas Biscayne Nature Center

H3 6767 Crandon Blvd, Key Biscayne biscaynenaturecenter.org

Overlooking the ocean at the north end of Crandon Park, this center

MIAMI VICE

September 16, 1984, was a day that altered Miami overnight. That evening *Miami Vice* debuted on TV, setting the stage for the city to conquer the world of high-profile glitz and hedonism. The slick, candy-colored world of edgy outlaws, fast cars, and deals caught the global imagination, and Miami was the place to be.

Cape Florida Lighthouse overlooking the ocean

contains a unique black mangrove reef of fossilized wood and roots. It is possible to wade in shallow waters to explore the underwater world with suitable foot protection on. The nature center is named after the woman who almost single-handedly saved the Everglades from being overrun by housing developments, and it offers information and guided tours.

9 The Wolfsonian-FIU

A museum and design research institute *(p36)* that traces the origins of Deco and other significant modern artistic trends.

10 Jewish Museum of Florida

R5 301 Washington Ave, South Beach 10am–4pm Wed–Sun jmof.fiu.edu

This fascinating museum chronicles the Jewish experience in Florida, with more than 100,000 items in the permanent collection. Highlights include a rare porcelain plate from 1865, an ornate ivory-covered Confirmation Bible printed in Vienna in 1911, and 19th-century community wedding rings from central Europe. Additional bonuses include concession stands, 75 barbecue grills, a pretty winding boardwalk, and convenient parking.

A WALK THROUGH THE ART DECO DISTRICT

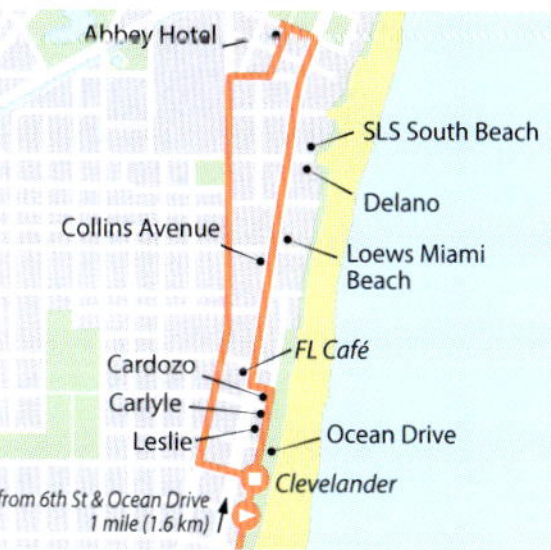

Morning

From the southern end of the District on **Ocean Drive**, at 6th Street, head northward, checking out not just the facades but also as many of the hotel interiors for the unique design elements in their lobbies, bars, and gardens. Between the **Leslie** and the **Cardozo** is the wonderful **Carlyle**. Turn left at 13th Street and walk to **Collins Avenue**. Turn right on Collins and stop for lunch at **FL Café** *(No. 1360 at 14th Street)*, set in an historic Art Deco building.

Afternoon

A little farther on, you'll find the **Loews Miami Beach** *(p148)*, which features a cut coral facade. At No. 1685, admire the all-white **Delano**, with its landmark winged tower. The outlandish Postmodern interiors were by Philippe Starck, and contain original Dali and Gaudi furniture. Next stop is the **SLS South Beach** *(p148)*, with another fantasy glass tower block. When you get to 21st Street, turn left; on the next corner you will encounter the Abbey Hotel, with its salamander motif and Flash Gordon-style towers. Retrace your steps and cap the walk with a drink at the **Clevelander** *(p90)*, a beautiful spot to end your day in the Art Deco District.

Kite-flying, a popular seaside pastime in Miami

Outdoor Activities

1. Swimming
Miles of coastline attract beach lovers to Florida, where swimming is one of the most popular activities (along with snorkeling) in quieter areas, especially Crandon Park on Key Biscayne *(p84)* and South Pointe.

2. Surfing and Windsurfing
For windsurfing in the area, the intracoastal waterways are calm and breezy; check out Miami Water Sports *(miamiwatersports.com)* for rentals. The Atlantic side offers great conditions for surfing.

3. Cycling
Cycling is the best way to explore both Miami Beach and Key Biscayne. For bike rental, gear, and accessories, the Miami Beach Bicycle Center *(bikemiami beach.com)* is a good starting point.

4. Jet-Skiing
Rentals are available at Hobie Island Beach and on the beaches at Virginia Key *(p55)*; weave through the waves and head for the horizon.

5. Workouts
South Pointe Park has a famous calisthenics circuit you can huff and puff your way through while taking in the views of Miami Beach.

6. Kite-Flying
This is a very popular activity, given the prevailing maritime winds. There's even a park especially for kite enthusiasts, which is located at the south end of Haulover Park.

7. Volleyball
Anywhere there's a developed beach you're likely to find a volleyball net and a quorum of players. Lummus Park is the best place to show off your skills to Miami's greatest beach bums, but South Pointe Park's a close contender.

8. Tennis
There are plenty of tennis courts available for rental throughout the area. Miami-Dade County Parks and Recreation Department *(miami dade.gov)* and Flamingo Park Tennis Center *(flamingotenniscenter.com)* offer good facilities.

9. Golf
Florida has over 1,000 golf courses – more than any other state – ranging from tournament-level courts to affordable public facilities. Many clubs are open to the public, with some offering scenic coastal views. The Crandon golf course *(golfcrandon.com)* on Key Biscayne is regarded as one of the best.

10. Fishing
Deep-sea fishing out in the ocean, or the more conventional kind off a jetty or pier – both are readily available. The South Pointe Park Pier on Miami Beach is good, or the breaker area just south of the Lighthouse on Key Biscayne.

Shopping

1. Collins Avenue from 6th to 9th Streets, South Beach

R4

This area has designer boutiques in ample supply including Armani Exchange, Studio 26, Frankie's Bikinis, and Free People. Also present are favorites such as Sunglass Hut, Shoe Palace, and Vans.

2. Runway Swimwear

R2 609 Lincoln Rd, South Beach runwayswimwear.com

Prepare for the beach by picking up the latest swimwear fashions for men and women here.

3. Bachi Jewels

S3 1627 Washington Ave, South Beach bachijewels.com

Popular with Miami Beach locals, this jewelry store stocks everything from cheap faux turquoise chains to custom-made diamond rings. It also offers repairs.

4. Lids

R2 521 Lincoln Rd, South Beach lids.com

With a large selection of sport apparel, fashion wear, and collegiate hats, Lids is the ideal place to buy gifts that won't take up much room in your suitcase.

5. Original Penguin

R2 925 Lincoln Rd, South Beach originalpenguin.com

Known for its bold prints and menswear, this iconic American sportswear brand is especially popular in Miami Beach.

6. Beach Bunny Swimwear

Q2 1006 Lincoln Rd, South Beach beachbunnyswimwear.com

Shop for ladies' swimwear, beach clothing, and accessories, including hats, sandals, and designer towels.

7. Art Deco Welcome Center

Besides a wealth of information about this historic district *(p24)*, you'll discover a treasure trove of Deco kitsch to take home as your very own. There's everything from cutesy salt and pepper sets to really rather nice reproduction lamps.

8. P448 Miami Beach

R3 420 Espanola Way, South Beach p448.com

Funky Italian footwear brand with street shoes and colorful sneakers. The store itself is worth a look inside for street art and colorful murals by local artists.

9. Ban de Osh

R2 816 Lincoln Rd, South Beach bandeosh.com

Mediterranean-inspired slow fashion store selling women's clothing, swimwear, and home accessories. Everything has a breezy, boho-chic vibe befitting of Miami Beach. This is a perfect place to pick up festival wear or a unique piece of funky jewelry to take home.

10. The Webster

S3 1220 Collins Ave, South Beach thewebster.com

Men's and women's fashions from top designers are available here, surrounded by Art Deco elements, vintage wallpapers, brass finishes, and art collections throughout the space.

Browsing the collection at The Webster

LGBTQ+ Venues

Distinctive facade of the Big Pink

1. Palace Bar

S3 1052 Ocean Dr, South Beach palacesouthbeach.com

The first LGBTQ+ restaurant and bar on Ocean Drive, in the heart of the Art Deco District. Popular for weekend drag shows, and varied menus.

2. Twist

R4 1057 Washington Ave, South Beach twistsobe.com

SoBe's largest LGBTQ+ venue, with seven bars in one, has something fun on every night. Happy hour 3–9pm daily.

3. Bar at Hotel Gaythering

Q2 1409 Lincoln Rd, South Beach gaythering.com

A congenial lounge bar with a laid-back atmosphere, where soft ambient music does not overpower conversation. It specializes in micro beers and craft cocktails. Large HD TVs play shows and sporting events.

4. The Betsy Hotel

S3 1440 Ocean Dr, South Beach thebetsyhotel.com

A beachfront boutique hotel that bills itself as a "community artistic oasis" and supports LGBTQ+ arts and events.

5. Nathan's Bar

R4 1216 Washington Ave, South Beach nathansbeach club.com

Owned by a former Twist mixologist, this bar with a retro decor was started in 2021. It features superb drag acts and serves a variety of cocktails.

6. Kill Your Idol

S3 222 Española Way, South Beach 305 534 1009

A statue of Bruce Lee hovers above the bar, and the Monday drag shows attract the biggest LGBTQ+ contingent.

7. 12th Street Beach

S3

Marked by fluttering rainbow-colored flags, this is SoBe's "semi-official" LGBTQ+ beach. It's located right in the middle of Lummus Park, the venue for Pride Festival and Winter Party.

8. Axel Beach Miami

1500 Collins Ave, South Beach axelhotels.com

This gay-friendly hotel chain has opened a branch only a few steps away from Miami Beach. The wonderful Tropical Deco interior is pure modern Miami.

9. Diva Royale Restaurant

R2 501 Lincoln Rd, South Beach dragqueenshow.com

Open from brunch to dinner, this restaurant hosts popular drag shows and events, with an impressive cocktail menu and a well-curated food menu.

10. Big Pink

R5 157 Collins Ave, Miami Beach 305 532 4700

This somewhat kitschy, retro diner-themed haunt is hard to miss thanks to the pink VW Beetles parked outside. The lengthy menu of comfort foods contains more than 200 items, and portions are huge.

Nightlife

1. Voodoo
S4 928 Ocean Dr, Miami Beach voodoo.miami
A lively club, Voodoo serves a wide range of drinks. It features decent house DJs, and is crowned by the Voodoo Rooftop & Hookah Lounge.

2. Basement
S1 2901 Collins Ave, Miami Beach basement miami.com
It is never a boring night at this buzzing nightclub founded by the legendary owner of Studio 54. The venue is popular with Miami's glitterati, who come here to dance, bowl, or skate at its mini ice skating rink.

3. MR JONES
S2 320 Lincoln Rd, South Beach mrjonesmiami.com
This late-night restaurant and club stays lively until 5am. It features hip-hop music.

4. Mynt
S2 1921 Collins Ave, South Beach myntlounge.com
Sample a tipple or two from the cocktail menu at this stylish night-spot that is frequented by a hip South Beach crowd.

5. Do Not Sit on the Furniture
R3 423 16th St, South Beach donotsitonthefurniture.com
Specializing in underground dance music, this popular club hosts well-known local and international DJs.

6. Watr at the 1 Rooftop
S1 1 Hotel, 2341 Collins Ave, South Beach 1hotels.com
Featuring a rooftop bar with ocean views and an eco-chic aesthetic, Watr serves cocktails made with sustainable ingredients. Reservations are required for non-hotel guests.

7. Exchange Miami
S3 1532 Washington Ave, South Beach 305 763 8264
This luxurious club has a decent roster of resident and celebrity guest DJs.

8. Nikki Beach Miami Beach
R5 1 Ocean Dr, South Beach nikkibeach.com/miami-beach
The several bars and dance floors here include upbeat Beach Club and, upstairs, the laidback Summer House.

9. LIV
H3 4441 Collins Ave, Miami Beach livnightclub.com
Located in the Fontainebleau Miami Beach, LIV is a massive, high-energy and exclusive dance club.

10. Bodega Taqueria y Tequila
Q3 1220 16th St, South Beach bodegataqueria.com
Known for its potent margaritas and other cocktails, this nightclub, lounge, and bar is also popular for its Mexican street-style tacos and burritos. Its extensive tequila collection, lineup of top DJs, and lively vibe make the Bodega a must-visit spot.

Partygoers on the dance floor at LIV

Al-fresco dining at Pelican Café

Sidewalk Cafés

1. Taste Bakery Cafe

R2 773 17th St, South Beach taste-bakery.com

Enjoy all-day breakfasts, salads, and sandwiches, with fresh juice, smoothies, or roasted coffee at this popular neighborhood bakery and café.

2. Front Porch Café

S3 1458 Ocean Dr, South Beach 305 531 8300

A popular South Beach breakfast and lunch spot, Front Porch also attracts smart crowds for dinner and during happy hours on its outdoor terrace.

3. Clevelander

S4 1020 Ocean Dr, South Beach

Facing the beach on the sidewalk, this always has something going on: listen to the live music, have something to eat, or just relax.

4. Pelican Café

S4 826 Ocean Dr, South Beach

Grab a seat on the outdoor patio and sample dishes such as fresh pastas and Mediterranean salads.

5. Mango's Tropical Café

S4 900 Ocean Dr at 9th St

Always hot, with a huge Floribbean menu. The action spills outside.

6. The Ocean Grill

S2 2001 Collins Ave, South Beach thesetaihotels.com

This beachfront restaurant serves artfully prepared southern European, American, and seafood classics cooked on a wood-fired grill.

7. Segafredo L'Originale

R2 1040 Lincoln Rd, South Beach sze-originale.com

Stylish Italian café offering tasty gelato, espresso, iced coffee, and Italian soft drinks such as Chinotto by day. It transforms into a hip bar at night.

8. Panther Coffee - Miami Beach

Q2 1875 Purdy Ave, South Beach panthercoffee.com

Miami's famous artisanal coffee producer roasts its beans in Wynwood and Little Haiti. A range of espresso drinks and pastries are on offer.

9. Cantina Beach

H4 455 Grand Bay Dr, Key Biscayne 305 365 4500

Dine on chicken enchiladas at this oceanfront restaurant in the Ritz-Carlton.

10. Wet Willie's

S4 760 Ocean Dr, South Beach

This bar attracts a young, post-beach crowd with its powerful frozen drinks with names such as Call-A-Cab.

Restaurants

PRICE CATEGORIES
For a three-course meal for one with half a bottle of wine (or equivalent meal), taxes, and extra charges.

$ under $35 **$$** $35–$70 **$$$** over $70

1. The Local House
R5 400 Ocean Dr, South Beach localhouse.com · $$
Order lobster mac & cheese or try the tofu poke bowl at this hidden gem.

2. Prime 112
R5 112 Ocean Dr, South Beach 305 532 8112 · $$$
The South Beach elite tuck into juicy steaks and excellent seafood served by waiters in butcher-stripe aprons.

3. Joe's Stone Crab
R5 11 Washington Ave, South Beach joestonecrab.com · $$
Expect gloriously sweet stone crabs and a notorious wait to get in. Also try Miami's best key lime pie.

4. Queen Miami Beach
R4 550 Washington Ave, South Beach queenmiamibeach.com · $$$
This Japanese restaurant, set inside the old Paris Theater, has a raw bar and serves great sushi and top-grade beef cuts sourced from small farms.

5. Fratelli la Bufala
R5 437 Washington Ave, South Beach flbmiami.com · $$
The best pizza in town is served at this South Beach Italian spot.

6. Stubborn Seed
R5 101 Washington Ave, South Beach stubbornseed.com · $$$
Owned by Jeremy Ford, a former *Top Chef* winner, this Michelin-starred restaurant offers an eight-course menu, desserts, and cocktails.

7. Puerto Sagua Restaurant
R4 700 Collins Ave, South Beach puerto-sagua-restaurant.foodjoyy.com · $
Traditional Cuban fare is what brings lines out the door here. Regulars swear by the *ropa vieja* and oxtail.

8. Pane e Vino
S2 1450 Washington Ave, South Beach paneevinomia.com · $$
Cozy Italian restaurant from Sicilian chef GianPaolo Ferrera, featuring candlelit tables, elegant decor, and tasty dishes with homemade pasta. Be sure to try Paolo's celebrated Cannolo Siciliano for dessert.

9. Barton G – The Restaurant
Q3 1427 West Ave, South Beach bartong.com/miami-beach · $$$
Popular with locals, Barton G serves American comfort food with a twist. The lush orchid garden is a great setting for a romantic meal.

10. Yuca 105
R5 1555 Washington Ave, South Beach yuca105.com · $$
The name "Yuca" stands for Young Urban Cuban Americans. One of South Florida's original upscale Cuban restaurants, it has Cuban-Peruvian cuisine, an extensive wine list, trendy decor, and live entertainment.

Entrance to The Local House

DOWNTOWN AND LITTLE HAVANA

For many visitors, this part of Miami is the most fascinating. Here along the Miami River is where it all started in the late 1800s, but it took the arrival of Cuban exiles from the 1950s on for Miami to come into its own. On these busy streets, the Cuban community still thrives in the south, and Latin American influence in Miami continues to grow.

Iconic Freedom Tower soaring above the city

1 Freedom Tower

N1 600 Biscayne Blvd, Downtown For renovations moadmdc.org

Built in 1925 in the Mediterranean Revival style, this Downtown landmark was inspired by the 800-year-old bell tower of Seville Cathedral. Once home to the now-defunct *Miami Daily News*, and in the 1960s a reception center to process Cubans fleeing Castro, the building was restored in 1988 to create a Cuban museum. Today, it houses the MDC Museum of Art + Design.

For places to stay in the area, see p149

2 David W. Dyer Federal Building

N1 NE 1st Ave, Downtown For renovations until early 2026

This imposing Neo Classical edifice, finished in 1931, once hosted high-profile trials, including that of Manuel Noriega, the former president of Panama, in 1990. The second-floor mural, *Law Guides Florida's Progress* was designed by Denman Fink, famous for his work in Coral Gables. It depicts Florida's evolution from a tropical backwater to one of America's most prosperous states.

Exhibits at the Phillip and Patricia Frost Museum of Science

3 Pérez Art Museum

G3 1103 Biscayne Blvd, Downtown 11am–6pm Fri–Mon, 11am–9pm Thu pamm.org

Set in lush gardens, this art museum showcases various international and local artworks. Designed by architects Herzog & de Meuron, its galleries feature temporary exhibitions in various media and a permanent collection including contemporary Cuban art donated to the museum by its well-known benefactor, Jorge M. Pérez.

4 Phillip and Patricia Frost Museum of Science

G3 1101 Biscayne Blvd, Downtown 10am–6pm daily frostscience.org

This museum relocated in 2017 when entrepreneur Phillip Frost donated $35 million to the site. Its campus houses an aquarium, a planetarium, and the North and West Wings. The latter hosts interactive exhibits on exploration of the Everglades, the human body and mind, the story of flight, and the latest innovations in technology.

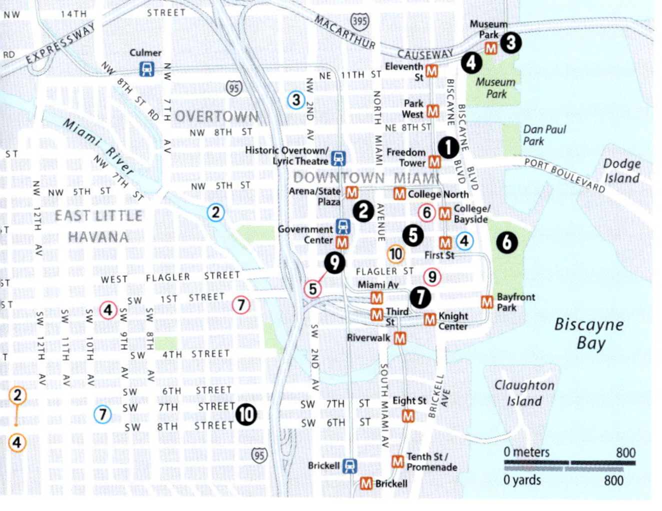

Intricately carved altars in the historic Gesu Church

5 Gesu Church

N1 118 NE 2nd St, Downtown
305 379 1424

This Mediterranean Revival building in the Spanish Colonial style, built in 1922, is the oldest Catholic church in Miami. It is known for its stunning stained-glass windows, ornate frescoes, and Italian-marble altars. One of its most remarkable features is the ceiling mural restored by a lone Nicaraguan refugee in the late 1980s.

6 Bayside Marketplace and Bayfront Park

P1–P2 401 Biscayne Blvd at 4th St, Downtown 10am–10pm Mon–Thu, 10am–11pm Fri & Sat, 11am–9pm Sun baysidemarketplace.com

Curving around Miamarina, this shopping and entertainment complex offers an undeniably fun-filled experience and is regarded as the best attraction in Downtown Miami. It's not South Beach, but La Vida Loca echoes here, too, often with live salsa bands playing on the esplanade. Shops – including Build-A-Bear, Victoria's Secret, Crocs, and Foot Locker – and 30 restaurants, with everything from ice cream to paella, make it a happening place. To the south, Bayfront Park, designed by Isamu Noguchi, is extensive and can provide a pleasant interlude of greenery, water, monuments, sculpture, and striking views.

7 Miami Tower

N2 100 SE 2nd St, Downtown

Built in 1983, this striking skyscraper is the work of architect I. M. Pei, famous for the glass pyramid in the courtyard of the Louvre in Paris. This building is notable both during the day for its Op-Art horizontal banding across the stepped hemi-cylinders, and at night for the changing colors of its overall illumination.

8 Cubaocho Museum

J3 1465 SW 8th St, Little Havana 10am–1am Wed & Thu, 11am–3am Fri & Sat, 1pm–1am Sun cubaocho.com

This cultural center celebrates the rich legacy of Cuban Americans. It was established by well-known art collector Roberto Ramos, who fled Cuba by boat in 1992. The museum's main

GATEWAY TO LATIN AMERICA

Two-thirds of Miami's population is of Hispanic origin. Pick up the *Miami Herald* and you'll see that the news of the day in Caracas, Bogotá, Managua, and – above all – Havana is given top billing. All these connections, for good or ill, have made Miami the US kingpin when it comes to dealing with Latin and South America.

gallery displays a permanent collection of pre-revolutionary Cuban artwork dating from the 1800s to the 1960s, including the famous 1937 painting *La Rumba* by Cuban painter Antonio Sánchez Araujo.

9 Miami-Dade Cultural Center

M2 101 W Flagler St, Downtown
Library: 10am–6pm Mon–Sat
Designed by celebrated American architect Philip Johnson in 1982, this Mediterranean-style complex is set around a tiled plaza and houses the interactive HistoryMiami *(p48)*, along with the Main Public Library, which contains more than four million books.

10 Calle Ocho and Around

The vibrant area around Calle Ocho (SW 8th Street) is a slice of Cuban culture, spiced up with all sorts of other Hispanic and Caribbean influences. Since Castro's Communist revolution in Cuba, Miami has become the main destination for wave after wave of immigrants fleeing the island that some still long for as home *(p28)*.

A row of shops and restaurants on Calle Ocho

A TRIP ALONG CALLE OCHO

Mid-morning

Cigar lovers should make the **Little Havana Cigar Factory** *(p29)* on SW 8th Street their first stop. Just across SW 15th Avenue you will find the **Cubaocho Museum**, which has an excellent collection of Cuban art. Come back later in the evening to catch a live performance, while enjoying a mojito at the bar. Next stop is SW 13th Avenue, to see the monuments to Cuban freedom fighters at the **Brigade 2506 Memorial Eternal Flame** *(p28)*, before a visit to the delightful fruit market at No. 1334, **Los Pinareños Fruteria** *(p98)*. Retrace your steps to the corner of SW 15th Avenue, peek in on **Domino Park** *(p29)*. Then take time to stop for coffee and a snack at the **La Colada**, on SW 8th at No. 1518.

Late morning

Continuing on to the next block, at No. 1652, take in the exciting Latin American art displayed at the **Taberna del Pintor Agustín Gaínza** *(p97)*, where you're likely to meet the artist himself. After that, try a free-form ramble of discovery – but don't miss the gaudy entrance to **La Casa de los Trucos** *(p98)*, at No. 1343. When it's time for lunch, head for **La Carreta** *(p99)*, on the south side of Calle Ocho, to enjoy good Cuban food at reasonable prices.

Walks and Viewpoints

Boats cruising along the Miami Riverwalk

1. Miami Riverwalk

This riverside promenade runs along the north bank of the Miami River and passes around the skyscrapers from Bayfront Park to the South West 2nd Street bridge.

2. Calle Ocho Walk

Stroll along Calle Ocho, between 12th and 17th avenues, where famous Latin American icons such as Gloria Estefan are honored with stars on the sidewalk *(p29)*. Along the same stretch, between 11th and 17th avenues, you can explore local shops and sample Cuban delicacies.

3. Bayside Marketplace

Adjacent to the impressive Miami-Dade Arena, this complex *(p94)* feels part Disney theme park, part international bazaar. Located right on the waterfront, it's always good for a late night stroll.

4. Architectural Walk

Even a short walk along the six blocks of NE–SE 1st and 2nd avenues is highly rewarding, offering a glimpse of buildings that showcase features of various styles, including chic, evocative signs, windows, and friezes. Just three blocks away, the Neo-Classical Revival Miami-Dade County Courthouse is also worth a visit. Don't miss the ceiling mosaics in the lobby.

5. A Ride on the Metromover

The free Metromover *(p141)* consists of two elevated loops running around Downtown, so it's a great way to get an overview of the area.

6. Views of Downtown

Some of the best views of Downtown can be seen from the city's freeways. As you cross MacArthur Causeway from South Beach, you can enjoy several dazzling perspectives, especially at night. For one of the finest views of the skyline, head to the Rickenbacker Causeway.

7. A Calle Ocho Café

El Rey De Las Fritas *(p99)* is the perfect spot to enjoy Cuban food and tasty island cocktails, all while watching the fascinating street life around it.

8. A Stroll in José Martí Park

This charming little park by the Miami River is graced with colonnades and pavilions, Spanish-style clusters of street lamps, palm trees, and an excellent children's playground.

9. A Stroll in Bayfront Park

Right on beautiful Biscayne Bay, this park was designed by Isamu Noguchi "as a wedge of art in the heart of the New World." In addition to Noguchi's sculptures, here you will find lush greenery, a small sand beach, tropical rock garden, cascading fountain, palms, and olive trees.

10. A Trip Through Little Havana

To get the overall feel and better understand the extent of Little Havana *(p28)*, head from José Martí Park in the west to 34th Avenue in the east, where you can find the Woodlawn Park North Cemetery and Versailles Restaurant.

Latin Arts Venues

1. Latin Art Core
J3 1646 SW 8th St latinartcore.com
This Calle Ocho art gallery showcases works by noted Latin American and Cuban artists, such as Ramon Alejandro and Perez Crespo.

2. Teatro 8
G3 2173 SW 8th St teatro8.com
Home to the Hispanic Theater Guild, Teatro 8 is known for its performances that celebrate Latin American culture.

3. Taberna del Pintor Agustín Gaínza
J3 1652 SW 8th St agustingainza.com
Admire the work of Cuban-born Agustín Gaínza, whose *oeuvre* covers every medium including painting, printmaking, ceramics, and recycled bottles.

4. Manuel Artime Theater
L2 900 SW 1st St miamigov.com/manuelartime
A former Baptist church, this building has been converted into an 800-seat theater and now serves as the home of the Miami Hispanic Ballet.

5. Pérez Art Museum Miami
This museum *(p93)* has a permanent collection of Cuban art. Look out for works by Cuban artist Wisredo Lamb.

6. MDC Live Arts
N1 Miami-Dade Community College, Wolfson Campus, 300 NE 2nd Ave, at NE 3rd St liveartsmiami.org
The Performance Series presents music, dance, film, and visual arts.

7. Miami Hispanic Cultural Art Center
L2 111 Southwest 5th Ave miamihispanicculturalartscenter.org
The Miami Hispanic Ballet Company, Cuban Classical Ballet of Miami, and Creation Art Center are based here.

8. Casa Juancho
G3 2436 SW 8th Ave casajuancho.com
This restaurant serves award-winning cuisine, as well as lively Spanish performances and a flamenco show.

9. Olympia Theater
N2 153 E Flagler St olympiatheater.org
This historic theater hosts a range of performances and film screenings during the annual Miami Film Festival.

10. Old's Havana
J3 1442 SW 8th St oldshavana.com
This lively Cuban bar and kitchen pays tribute to vintage Havana and hosts regular live entertainment.

Stunning glass facade of the Pérez Art Museum

Cuban/Latin Shopping

Colorful artwork on display at Taberna del Pintor Gaínza

1. Taberna del Pintor Gaínza

This gallery *(p97)* is named after the celebrated Cuban artist whose work is on display here along with that of other contemporary Cuban and Latin American artists.

2. La Casa de los Trucos

K3 1343 SW 8th St 305 858 5029

A must-visit for all your costuming needs, this place features the most traditional as well as the most bizarre costumes. It has a vast inventory to buy or rent, with reasonable prices.

3. Little Havana Visitor Center

J3 1600 SW 8th St
305 643 5500

Little Havana Visitor Center is a unique gift shop and gallery selling Cuban souvenirs, apparel and various kinds of accessories. It is also home to the only Coca-Cola memorabilia shop in all of Miami.

4. Los Pinareños Fruteria

K3 1334 SW 8th St 305 285 1135

A delightful fruit market with all sorts of Caribbean produce, such as mamey and small "apple" bananas.

5. The Havana Shirt Store

J3 1421 SW 8th St 786 717 7474

This family-owned store is the place to buy traditional *guayabera* Cuban shirts in a variety of fabrics, along with Panama hats, linen shorts, and shoes.

6. Sentir Cubano

G3 3100 SW 8th St
sentircubano.com

Look for the vivid murals painted on the side of the building and you'll know you've arrived at this crazy store loaded with Cuban memorabilia.

7. Versailles Bakery

G3 3501 SW 8th St
versaillesbakery.com

Delicious homemade pastries will satisfy your sweet tooth, plus desserts like flan and cheesecake accompanied by Cuban coffee.

8. Little Havana Gift Shop

J3 1522 SW 8th St 786 768 1170

This little shop has a wide range of Cuban-themed souvenirs on display including T-shirts, hats, wooden sculptures, and paintings.

9. Little Havana Cigar Factory

Enjoy the finest cigars money can buy *(p28)*. Expert staff are happy to make personalized recommendations.

10. Seybold Building

N2 36 NE 1st St 305 374 7922

This multistory building is home to several high-end stores, offering jewelry and watches, alongside both wholesale and retail shops. The prices are good value and with so many choices, you will have a hard time deciding what to buy.

Places to Eat

PRICE CATEGORIES

For a three-course meal for one with half a bottle of wine (or equivalent meal), taxes, and extra charges.

$ under $35 **$$** $35–$70 **$$$** over $70

1. Versailles Restaurant

G3 3555 SW 8th St, at SW 35th Ave versaillesrestaurant.com · $$

A Little Havana institution, Versailles Restaurant is actually a Cuban diner in a very sleek guise.

2. Garcia's Seafood Grille & Fish Market

L1 398 NW North River Dr garciasmiami.com · $$

This family-run restaurant with a friendly atmosphere is known for its delicious grouper chowder and conch steak. Note, there's often a short wait.

3. Red Rooster

M2 920 NW 2nd Ave, Overtown redroosterovertown.com · $$

The Red Rooster offers an eclectic menu that features a mix of Haitian specialties alongside Southern classics.

4. CVI.CHE 105

P1 105 NE 3rd Ave ceviche105.com · $$

Chic Peruvian restaurant displaying eclectic artwork, and helmed by Juan Chipoco, who is well known for his tasty, fresh, and zesty ceviches.

5. El Rey De Las Fritas

J3 1821 SW 8th St elreydelasfritas.com · $

This no-frills Cuban diner specializes in Cuban-style burgers known as *fritas* prepared with ground beef patty, sautéed onions, thinly sliced fried potatoes, and a special sauce.

6. La Carreta

G3 3632 SW 8th St lacarreta.com · $

From the food to the clientele, this family restaurant in the heart of Little Havana is thoroughly Cuban. Good food at reasonable prices ensures its popularity. Open until late, the restaurant also offers takeout options.

7. Café la Trova

K3 971 SW 8th St cafelatrova.com · $$

Enjoy traditional Cuban dishes from chef Michelle Bernstein at this café, alongside artisanal cocktails.

8. Guayacan

J3 1933 SW 8th St guayacanmiami.com · $$

Cozy and unpretentious, Guayacan offers Cuban fare with a Nicaraguan twist. Try the *pescado a la Tipitapa* (red snapper served with sauce).

9. Sanguich

G3 2057 SW 8th St sanguich.com · $

With elegant decor, this place serves delicious Cuban classics at great prices.

10. El Cristo

J3 1543 SW 8th St elcristorestaurant.com · $

This old-fashioned restaurant set in the heart of Little Havana serves up classic Cuban dishes such as *ropa vieja* and *arroz con pollo*.

Patrons waiting in line at La Carreta

NORTH OF DOWNTOWN

There are plenty of reasons to set out beyond the confines of the central districts and explore Miami's outer neighborhoods. The areas north of Miami Beach and Downtown might not be as famous as the central hubs, but there are countless local delights to be discovered here. Some of Greater Miami's most fascinating historic sights, including one of the oldest buildings in the Americas, a thriving arts scene, and a range of fine dining options are all well worth seeking out. Wynwood Arts District is home to a vibrant street art scene and an array of eclectic galleries, bars, and restaurants. Bal Harbour and the North Beaches offer relative respite from the crowds of South Beach, and near the latter is the impressively reconstructed Ancient Spanish Monastery.

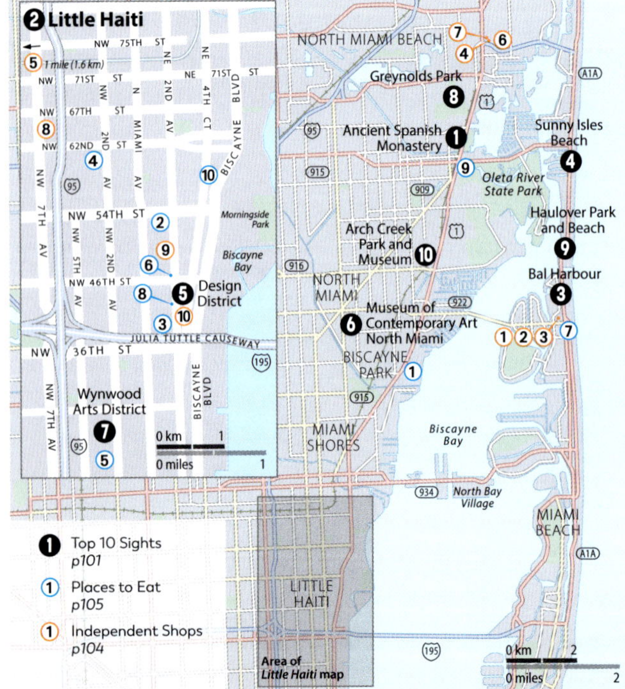

For places to stay in this area, see p150

Courtyard of the Ancient Spanish Monastery

1 Ancient Spanish Monastery

H1 16711 W Dixie Hwy, North Miami Beach Hours vary, check website spanishmonastery.com

This monastery is the oldest European-tradition building in the Western Hemisphere, originally built in 1133–41 near Segovia, Spain. In 1925, William Randolph Hearst bought the magnificent cloisters, had them dismantled stone by stone, and sent to the US, where the stones were reassembled in the early 1950s for $1.5 million. Check the website before visiting on weekends as the monastery remains closed for events such as weddings.

2 Little Haiti

G2 NE 2nd Ave, from about NE 55th to NE 80th

Many Haitians have settled here since the 1980s. The Little Haiti Cultural Complex, housed in the Caribbean Marketplace, is the heart of the community. The building has brightly colored ironwork inspired by the Iron Market in Port-au-Prince, Haiti. Further south in the Design District is the Haitian Heritage Museum *(haitianheritagemuseum.org)*.

3 Bal Harbour

H2

The Barrier Islands north of Miami Beach are occupied mainly by luxury residential areas. Known for its extravagant hotels and one of the swankiest malls, Bal Harbour is said to have more millionaires per capita than any other city in the US. On Collins Avenue, Bal Harbour Shops is particularly fancy. Elsewhere along 96th Street are galleries, gourmet shops, and many plastic surgery studios.

4 Sunny Isles Beach

H1 Hwy A1A (north of Haulover Park)

An ideal destination for both relaxation and adventure, Sunny Isles Beach offers serene beaches along with activities such as parasailing, paddle-boarding, and snorkeling. The resort is lined with high-rise hotels and condos, all built along the beachfront. Landmark buildings include the residential Porsche Design Tower and its high-tech robotic parking garage. The area has a large expat Russian community, with caviar shops and Russian delis, restaurants, beauty salons, and real estate companies underscoring the area's nickname "Little Moscow."

5 Design District

G2 Nr Buena Vista between NE 36th–41st sts and from NE 2nd to N Miami aves miamidesigndistrict.net

It started out as a pineapple grove, but from the 1920s this zone was being called Decorators' Row because of the design stores that had moved in. For a while in the 1980s, due to high crime, the area fell on hard times, but things improved, and top-end design, furniture, and fixture shops once again rule. Most artists have moved here to escape the high rents of South Beach.

6 Museum of Contemporary Art North Miami

G2 770 NE 125th St Noon–7pm Wed, 10am–5pm Thu–Sun mocanomi.org

The Museum of Contemporary Art opened its state-of-the-art building in 1996. It's known for its provocative exhibitions and for seeking a fresh approach in examining the art of our time. The permanent collection features emerging and established artists from the US and abroad.

7 Wynwood Arts District

G3 Bounded by N 36th St, N 20th St, I-95, and NW 1st Ave wynwoodmiami.com

The former industrial warehouse district of Wynwood has been transformed into a vibrant neighborhood of art galleries, museums, clubs, and studios. Since 2009, huge murals – dubbed the Wynwood Walls (*p76*) – have been a major element of the district's appeal.

8 Greynolds Park

H1 17530 W Dixie Hwy Sunrise–sunset daily miamidade/parks/greynolds

An oak-shaded haven for runners, golfers, and other outdoor enthusiasts, Greynolds Park is landscaped with native and non-native plants, which include mangrove, royal palm, sea grape, palmetto, pampas grass, and gumbo limbo. The park features several walking and biking trails, scenic views of the Oleta river, and

DOWNTOWN MIAMI

Visitors to Greater Miami will notice both its serious wealth and extreme poverty, often displayed within a stone's throw of each other. Many underserved African American communities, as well as struggling immigrants from places like Cuba, Haiti, and other Central American countries, endure substandard living conditions in quarters of endless urban blight.

Relaxing on the green at Greynolds Park

opportunities for birdwatching. You'll also find beach volleyball courts, a kids' playground, and plenty of picnic tables.

9 Haulover Park and Beach

H1 10800 Collins Ave 305 944 3040

Haulover Park contains one of south Florida's most beautiful beaches – a mile and a half (1 km) of golden sand drawing people from all walks of life. Nestled between the Intercoastal Waterway and the Atlantic, the beach is ideal for surfing and swimming, and on warm weekends it is jam-packed with sunbathers. The park itself has a marina, restaurant, tennis courts, a nine-hole golf course, and a kite shop. It is one of the nation's top ten nude beaches.

10 Arch Creek Park and Museum

G2 1855 NE 135th St

Created around a natural limestone bridge formation, this location stands on ground that was once an important Indigenous peoples trail. A museum contains artifacts left by Tequesta and Seminole peoples. Take a guided eco-tour to learn about endemic species.

Detailed murals in Wynwood Arts District

A TOUR OF THE ANCIENT SPANISH MONASTERY

Morning

Drive north from central Miami on Highway 1 (also known as Biscayne Boulevard). Turn left on NE 163rd Street, then right onto W Dixie Highway (also NE 22nd Avenue). The **Ancient Spanish Monastery** *(p101)* is on the right after the canal. You may well feel a sense of awe as you walk around this beautiful site. Even European visitors, who will no doubt have visited many such buildings in their homeland, marvel at Hearst's dedication to put it here. For the best route through the grounds, start at the museum, exit to the patio, then head through the gardens, cloisters, and rooms, ending at the chapel. Among the notable sights along the route are a 12th-century birdbath, a statue of the Spanish king Alphonso VII (the monastery was constructed to commemorate one of his victories over the Moors), and two of only three known surviving round stained-glass windows, also from the 12th century.

Afternoon

In keeping with the Spanish theme, eat at nearby **Paquito's Mexican Restaurant** *(p105)* and take a detour along NE 2nd Avenue through **Little Haiti** *(p101)* on your way back.

Independent Shops

1. Johanna Ortiz

H2 Bal Harbour Shops, 9700 Collins Ave 332 277 0672

Inspired by her Latin American roots, Johanna Ortiz's outfits feature elegant designs that are crafted organically and sustainably. Ortiz's brand is known for its tropical motifs.

2. Addict

H2 Bal Harbour Shops, 9700 Collins Ave 305 864 1099

Fashion sneakers for all the family, including rare sneakers not widely available in department stores.

3. 100% Capri

H2 Bal Harbour Shops, 9700 Collins Ave 305 866 4117

This Italian boutique's first US location offers a curated collection of luxury linen wear for men, women, and children, along with a fine selection of homeware.

4. Psycho Bunny

H1 Aventura Mall, 19565 Biscayne Blvd

This popular New York menswear brand with a captivating name has a huge cult following. The branch located in Aventura Mall sells its trademark polos, T-shirts, and hoodies.

Earthen pots from Jalan Jalan

5. Art By God

G3 1280 NW 74th St artbygod.com

Impressive mineral/nature store, with dinosaur fossils, natural and carved semi-precious gemstones, insects, shells, butterflies, skulls, animal mounts, and more.

6. Rebel

G2 7648 Biscayne Blvd 305 793 4104

Shoppers are bound to find something they want at Rebel, a high-end boutique that carries everything from everyday fashion to evening dresses.

7. Nini & Loli

H1 Aventura Mall, 19501 Biscayne Blvd niniandloli.com

This local Miami store specializes in baby gear, strollers, car seats, furniture, diaper bags, toys, apparel, and all the baby basics.

8. Rasool's Menswear

G2 6301 NW 7th Ave 305 759 1250

Famous for its sleek Italian suits for men, the store also stocks urban wear, wedding tuxedos, and T-shirts with creative artwork on them.

9. Upper Buena Vista

G2 184 NE 50th Terrace 305 539 9555

An indoor-outdoor shopping mall with plant-filled home decor stores, local artisan shops, and plenty of cafés to keep you fueled.

10. Jalan Jalan

G2 3600 NE 2nd Ave 305 572 9998

The owners constantly change this home design showroom to add global artisan pieces made of petrified wood, Belgian glass, and Indian marble work. It offers a great collection of art, home furnishings, and accessories.

Places to Eat

PRICE CATEGORIES

For a three-course meal for one with half a bottle of wine (or equivalent meal), taxes, and extra charges.

$ under $35 $$ $35–$70 $$$ over $70

1. Blue Runner Seafood

G2 Biscayne Blvd and 114th St
786 499 9334 · $

This Blue Runner seafood truck – one of only two in the city – serves up the best Gulf-caught oysters, crab, mahi, tuna, snapper, and swordfish, along with the freshest ceviche in town.

2. Chez Le Bebe

G2 114 NE 54th St
305 751 7639 · $

A Little Haiti spot serving traditional Haitian food, from tender *griot* (pork) to stewed goat; dishes come with rice, beans, plantain, and salad.

3. Michael's Genuine Food and Drink

G2 130 NE 40th St 305 676 0894 · $$

The best restaurant in Miami's Design District has a unique menu, serving a range of fresh seafood dishes, wood-fired pizzas, and tempting cocktails.

4. Clive's Cafe

G2 5890 NW 2nd Ave 305 757 6512 · $

A popular Jamaican restaurant in the heart of Little Haiti, serving delicious classics such as jerk chicken and curry goat, as well as salt fish for breakfast.

5. Panther Coffee

G3 2390 NW 2nd Ave 305 677 3952 · $

Miami's wildly popular small-batch coffee roaster operates this café in the Wynwood Arts District, with local art on the walls and a menu of cakes, cookies, and savory snacks.

Pretty patio at the Mandolin Aegean Bistro

6. Lemoni Café

G2 4600 NE 2nd Ave 305 571 5080 · $

Cozy Design District café serving wholesome food with a Mediterranean slant, which is influenced by the chef's French/Moroccan background.

7. Josh's Deli

H2 1000 E 16th St 305 576 3945 · $

This classic New York-style deli in Surfside serves both familiar and lesser-known comfort food, including pastrami, lox, *latkes*, matzo ball soup, and tender corned beef sandwiches.

8. Mandolin Aegean Bistro

G2 4312 NE 2nd Ave 305 749 9140 · $$

This stylish Design District bistro recreates simple, rustic dishes from Greece and Turkey.

9. Paquito's Mexican Restaurant

G1 16265 Biscayne Blvd 786 321 4952 · $$

Expect fresh tortilla soup, steak Paquitos sautéed in a jalapeño and onion sauce, and a yummy *mole verde*.

10. Andiamo!

G2 5600 Biscayne Blvd
305 762 5751 · $

Mouthwatering, brick-oven pizza pies, as well as salads, paninis, and a selection of local beers.

CORAL GABLES AND COCONUT GROVE

Together, Coral Gables and Coconut Grove constitute one of the most upscale neighborhoods in Greater Miami. Among the first and most successful planned suburbs in the US, Coral Gables was built by the real-estate developer George Merrick. Known as the "City Beautiful," it earns its moniker from its winding avenues lined with elegant villas. Luxurious mansions and sailboats anchored in Biscayne Bay typify affluent Coconut Grove, where dining at a sidewalk café is a quintessential experience. This area has been constantly evolving since the countercultural days of the 1960s, and today its lively street scene makes it one of Miami's most vibrant districts.

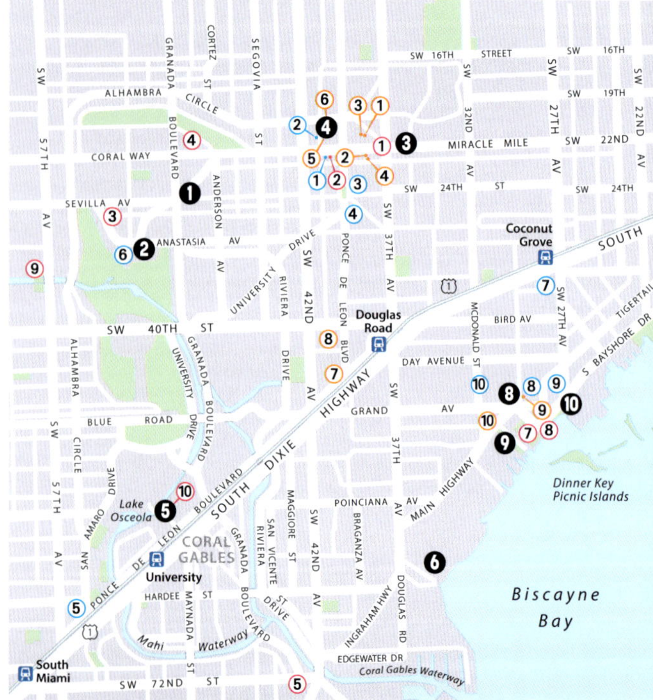

For places to stay in this area, see p151

George Merrick's picturesque Venetian Pool

1 Venetian Pool

G3 · 2701 De Soto Blvd, Coral Gables · Hours vary seasonally, check website · Dec–Feb & national hols · coralgables.com

This is one of the loveliest and most evocative of Merrick's additions to his vision for Coral Gables. Fed by natural springs, the pool served as a filming location for a movie starring the famous American swimmer and actress, Esther Williams.

2 The Biltmore

One of the grandest hotels in Florida, the fabulous Biltmore complex *(p151)* was built in the Spanish Revival style and features a tower inspired by the Giralda in Seville. Herculean pillars line the lobby, and from the terrace you can survey the largest hotel swimming pool in the country. American swimmer and actor Johnny Weissmuller, best known for portraying Tarzan in 12 films between 1932 and 1948, once taught swimming here. The likes of Al Capone, Judy Garland, and the Roosevelts also frequented this hotel in its heyday. Weekly tours of the hotel and grounds depart from the front desk.

3 Miracle Mile

F3–G3 · Coral Way between Douglas and Le Jeune rds

In 1940, a developer hyped the "City Beautiful's" main shopping street by naming it Miracle Mile. Today, colorful canopies adorn the shops, boutiques and restaurants here. Stop to admire the Colonnade Building, now the Hotel Colonnade, with its striking rotunda, fountain, and Corinthian columns. Just a short stroll away on Aragon Avenue, you will find the Old Police and Fire Station, now home to the Coral Gables Museum *(p108)*.

Vizcaya
Alice Wainwright Park
Rickenbacker Cwy
South Miami Av
Dixie Highway
S Miami Av
Brickell Av
Grove Isle
Kennedy Park

0 km 1
0 miles 1

❶ Top 10 Sights p107
① Places to Eat p113
① Boutiques p112
① The Best of the Rest p110

4 Coral Gables Museum

G3 285 Aragon Ave, Coral Gables 11am–5pm Tue–Fri & Sun, 10am–6pm Sat coralgablesmuseum.org

This fascinating museum chronicles the evolution of Coral Gables over time and Merrick's contribution to the area. The museum also features displays on Miami's rich historical and architectural heritage. Permanent exhibits include a remarkable display on the Tamiami Trail *(p134)*, which addresses the highway's devastating impact on the Everglades. Other highlights include the Carole A. Fewell Gallery and the expansive public courtyard near the main lobby.

Commodore Munroe's house, Barnacle Historic State Park

5 Lowe Art Museum

With around 19,500 pieces, Greater Miami's finest art museum *(p34)* features collections of both ancient and modern world art.

6 The Kampong

G4 4013 Douglas Rd For tours, check website ntbg.org

Just southwest of Coconut Grove, the Kampong is one of Miami's lesser-visited attractions. This botanical garden was created by explorer and horticulturist David Fairchild. He bought the estate in 1916, spending the next 40 years developing a collection of more than 5,000 tropical flowers, fruit trees, and plants, with an emphasis on Asia. The site includes the Fairchild-Sweeney House, built in 1928 in a combination of Spanish and Southeast Asian styles. Book your visit in advance via the website.

Arched gateway to the garden, The Kampong

7 Vizcaya Museum and Gardens

An icon of the city's cultural life, this historic museum *(p30)* features scenic formal gardens that are perfect for a leisurely walk.

8 CocoWalk

G3 3015 Grand Ave cocowalk.com

A five-story retail and entertainment venue in the heart of Coconut Grove, CocoWalk features 150,000 sq ft (14,000 sq m) of shops, restaurants, and entertainment spots. The atmosphere here is that of a village, with people hanging out, zipping by on in-line skates and bikes, or clustering around the landscaped outdoor plaza where live music performances are often held. The main attractions in the evenings are the hip bars and the large multiplex cinema.

9 Barnacle Historic State Park

G3 3485 Main Hwy, Coconut Grove Munroe House Museum: For tours 10am, 11:30am, 1pm, & 2:30pm Fri–Wed; grounds: 9am–5pm Fri–Wed floridastateparks.org

This park is centered around Dade County's oldest home, the Barnacle, now known as the Munroe House Museum. Built in 1891 by Commodore Ralph Munroe, a boat builder and wrecker (salvager), the residence houses family heirlooms, old tools, and wonderfully dated appliances, such as one of the first refrigerators.

10 Dinner Key

G3 5 Bayshore Dr

The name of this marina complex derives from the early days when settlers had picnics here. In the 1930s, Pan American Airways transformed Dinner Key into the busiest seaplane base in the US. It was also the departure point for Amelia Earhart's doomed round-the-world flight in 1937. You can still see the airline's sleek Streamline Moderne terminal, housing the Miami City Hall; the hangars where seaplanes were harbored are now mostly boatyards. The marina here is the most prestigious in Miami, and berths many luxurious yachts.

A TOUR OF COCONUT GROVE VILLAGE

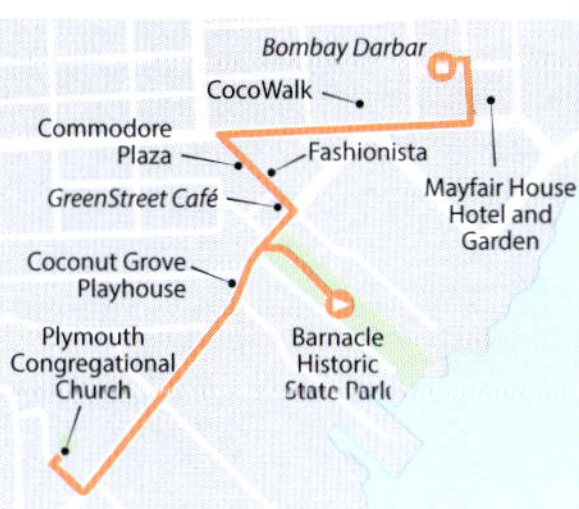

Morning

Begin your day with the 10am tour of the **Barnacle Historic State Park** (note, it's closed on Thursdays). As you exit, turn left and go down to the corner of Devon Road to the **Plymouth Congregational Church** (*plymouthmiami.org*), built in 1916. If they're open, pop into the back gardens. Walk back along Main Highway to the **Coconut Grove Playhouse** (*No. 3500*), which, although not used, is a handsome Mediterranean Revival building. Continue along Main Highway to the next street, then stop for lunch at the ever-busy **GreenStreet Café** (*p111*).

Afternoon

After lunch, walk up **Commodore Plaza** to visit **Fashionista** (*p112*). Afterward, continue on to Grand Avenue and turn right. Walk a few blocks to the main intersection then cross the street to reach **CocoWalk**, a shopper's paradise. On the next block, Rice Street, look up to admire the fanciful facade of **Mayfair House Hotel and Garden** (*mayfairhousemiami.com*). Finish your tour with dinner at the nearby Indian restaurant **Bombay Darbar** (*p113*), known for its delicious curries and tasty kebabs.

Tropical waters of Matheson Park

The Best of the Rest

1. Merrick Villages

Driving around Coral Gables to take in these luxury residences *(p24)*, done up in various styles, will take a couple of leisurely hours.

2. Actors' Playhouse

G3 280 Miracle Mile, Coral Gables actorsplayhouse.org

One of South Florida's largest theaters, the Actors' Playhouse runs an eclectic mix of plays for adults and children.

3. Church of the Little Flower

G3 2711 Indian Mound Trail, Coral Gables cotlf.org

Celebrated for its Mediterranean Revival architecture, this church hosts an excellent choir, and has long been a gathering place for the community.

4. Coral Gables Merrick House

G3 907 Coral Way, Coral Gables 305 774 0155 For tours: 1pm, 2pm, & 3pm Sat & Sun

The restored boyhood home of George Merrick is remarkably modest compared to the grandeur of the dreams he realized. The city of Coral Gables took its name from this house. This historic site is now a museum with exhibits on Coral Gables and its surrounding area.

5. Matheson Park

G3 9610 Old Cutler Road

This park has a small human-made atoll pool, which is flushed naturally with water from Biscayne Bay.

6. Congregational Church

G3 3010 De Soto Blvd, Coral Gables 305 448 7421 For services: 9am & 11am Sun

Merrick's Baroque paean to his father, a Congregational minister, was Coral Gables' first church and remains the city's most beautiful to this day.

7. Peacock Park

G3

With superb views over Biscayne Bay, Peacock Park offers a host of recreational activities including basketball courts and soccer fields.

8. Coconut Grove Sailing Club

G3 2990 Bayshore Drive cgsc.org

Learn to take to the waters like a pro with some of the city's best sailing lessons, on offer at this esteemed boating club.

9. Coral Gables Wayside Park

G3

This small green space, intersected by a canal, is home to two square towers originally constructed in the 1920s.

10. Coconut Grove Village

G3

With a vibrant community centered around CocoWalk *(p108)*, this charming area is perfect for a stroll. The outdoor mall is one of the most popular destinations, with a courtyard full of brilliant cafés and souvenir stalls.

Special Places and Events

1. Grove Tree lighting

First weekend in Dec

The annual lighting of the Coconut Grove Christmas tree marks the first festive event of the season.

2. Titanic Brewing Company

This popular Coral Gables brewpub *(p113)* offers six styles of house brews on tap, along with 25 varieties of seasonal beers. It also hosts regular live music performances.

3. Watsco Center

G3 1245 Dauer Dr, Coral Gables watscocenter.com

This modern multi-purpose arena in the University of Miami campus seats 8,000 for a variety of recreational events, from college basketball to rock concerts.

4. GreenStreet Café

G3 3468 Main Hwy, Coconut Grove 305 444 0244

Almost always crowded, this corner venue on Commodore Plaza is a prime people-watching spot in the Grove.

5. Beaux Arts Festival of Art

beauxartsmiami.org

This lively exhibition of local art is held annually, usually in January.

6. King Mango Strut

Late Dec–Early Jan kingmango strut.org

This outrageous tradition dates back to when the Grove was a haven for intellectuals and eccentrics. The festivities begin at the Main Highway and Commodore Plaza, culminating in a concert and dance at Peacock Park.

7. Tamiami International Orchid Festival

Jan tamiamiorchid festival.com

Florida has become one of the world centers for the orchid industry. More than half a million pretty blooms are exhibited at the Miami-Dade County Fair Expo Center *(fairexpo.com)*, with different themes every year.

8. Coconut Grove Arts Festival

Third weekend in Feb cgaf.com

This festival, centered around Coconut Grove, hosts all manner of events. Visitors flock to the area to enjoy food, drinks, live concerts, and a variety of arts and crafts booths.

9. Miami-Bahamas Goombay Festival

Mid-May/early Jun coconutgrove bahamiangoombayfestival.com

Coconut Grove comes alive for the biggest African American heritage festival in the US. The party includes a vibrant parade, Caribbean music, island food, and *junkanoo* dancers.

10. Columbus Day Regatta

Mid-Oct columbusdayregatta.net

Some 600 boats take part in this fun sailing race from the Coral Reef Yacht Club *(coralreefyacht club.org)* to Elliot Key in Biscayne National Park *(p117)*.

Stalls set up for the Columbus Day Regatta

Boutiques

1. Golden Triangle

G3 2308 Galiano St, Coral Gables
caffeabbracci.com

A New Age boutique offering imported items from Asia including incense, Tibetan bowls, and Buddha statues.

2. Morays Jewelers

G3 116 Miracle Mile, Coral Gables
moraysjewelers.com

Shop for watches, diamonds, pearls, and gemstone pieces at Morays.

3. Zoey Reva

G3 133 Giralda Ave, Coral Gables
zoeyreva.com

A hidden gem in Coral Gables. Great selection of stylish women's clothing, with a fabulous line in patterned dresses and loungewear.

4. Essence Boutique

G3 78 Miracle Mile, Coral Gables
essencemiami.com

High-quality women's attire, including purses, shoes, swimwear, and jewelry.

5. Pepi Bertini

G3 357 Miracle Mile, Coral Gables
pepibertini.com

Started in 1985 by Cuban-born Pepi "Bertini" Gonzalez, this bespoke Italian-style tailor shop deals in menswear.

6. Books and Books

G3 265 Aragon Ave, Coral Gables
booksandbooks.com

One of a chain of stores across the state, this bookshop specializes in arts and literature, and books on Florida. Here there's a great café, frequent poetry readings, and book signings.

7. White House Black Market

G3 350 San Lorenzo Ave, Suite 2130 whitehouseblackmarket.com

Known for its elegant cocktail dresses, tailored suits, shoes, and accessories.

8. Vuori

G3 358 San Lorenzo Ave
vuoriclothing.com

Inspired by the coastal California lifestyle, Vuori offers athletic and performance clothing including fitness, surf, and sportswear.

9. The Maya Hatcha

G3 2982 Grand Ave, Coconut Grove mayahatcha.com

This boho shop sells ethically made clothing and handmade jewelry.

10. Fashionista

G3 3135 Commodore Plaza, Coconut Grove shopthefashionista.com

This is the place to pick up designer merchandise, albeit slightly worn, for a fraction of the price.

Literary-themed café at Books and Books

Places to Eat

PRICE CATEGORIES

For a three-course meal for one with half a bottle of wine (or equivalent meal), taxes, and extra charges.

$ under $35 **$$** $35–$70 **$$$** over $70

1. Kaia Greek Earth Grill

G3 232 Miracle Mile, Coral Gables 786 362 6997 · **$$**

Savor flavorful Mediterranean cuisine in a breezy dining area decorated with wicker and woodwork. Try the delicious grilled octopus, calamari, hummus, and the tasty cocktails.

2. Caffe Abbracci

G3 318 Aragon Ave, Coral Gables caffeabbracci.com · **$$$**

Founded by restaurateur Nino Pernetti, this spot offers a Mediterranean ambience and Italian comfort food. The menu has a variety of desserts.

3. Pascal's on Ponce

G3 2611 Ponce de Leon Blvd, Coral Gables pastoratpascal.net · **$$$**

A perfect place for a romantic meal, Pascal's on Ponce serves French classics prepared by chef Pascal Oudin.

4. Christy's

G3 3101 Ponce de Leon Blvd, Coral Gables christysrestaurant.com · **$$$**

A local favorite since its opening in 1978, this restaurant is frequented by politicians, CEOs, and celebrities.

5. Titanic Brewing Company

G3 5813 Ponce de Leon Blvd, Coral Gables titanicbrewery.com · **$**

Lift a pint of homemade brew and sample crawfish or calamari snacks.

6. Fontana

F3 1200 Anastasia Ave, Coral Gables 855 311 6903 · **$$$**

A fine dining experience unlike no other, led by renowned chef Giuseppe "Beppe" Galazzi. The restaurant's beautiful fountain and Mediterranean architecture offer a stunning backdrop for an enjoyable meal.

Beautifully landscaped courtyard at Fontana

7. Berries in the Grove

G3 2884 SW 27th Ave, Coconut Grove berriesinthegrove.com · **$$**

Locals have embraced this restaurant, which captures the best of Florida's sunshine and healthy cuisine – from a pizza to a tropical fruit smoothie.

8. Bombay Darbar

G3 2901 Florida Ave, Coconut Grove bombaydarbar.com · **$$**

Regarded as Miami's best Indian restaurant. The menu has kebabs, curries, and vegetarian options.

9. Isabelle's Coconut Grove

G3 3300 SW 27th Ave, Coconut Grove isabellescoconutgrove.com · **$$$**

Located in the Ritz Carlton, this gourmet restaurant specializes in seafood. Try the sandwiches, mushroom pappardelle, or Florida snapper.

10. Le Bouchon du Grove

G3 3430 Main Hwy, Coconut Grove lebouchondugrove.net · **$$$**

Transporting diners to France for over 20 years, this cozy bistro is renowned for its traditional Lyonnaise cuisine. It serves breakfast, lunch, and dinner.

SOUTH OF COCONUT GROVE

Heading south from Miami's main attractions, once you get past the vast and sprawling suburbs, you enter tracts of citrus groves and tropical nurseries. The general atmosphere changes, too – a bit more traditional and Old South. There is a wide range of museums, parks, and gardens here, which often double as educational attractions for kids and adults alike. While sights like the Gold Coast Railroad Museum and Charles Deering Estate provide a glimpse into South Florida's rich history, others such as the Fairchild Tropical Botanic Garden and the Montgomery Botanical Center focus on ecology and the conservation of tropical plants. There's also the Biscayne National Park, a veritable marine wonderland teeming with aquatic life and perfect for watersports.

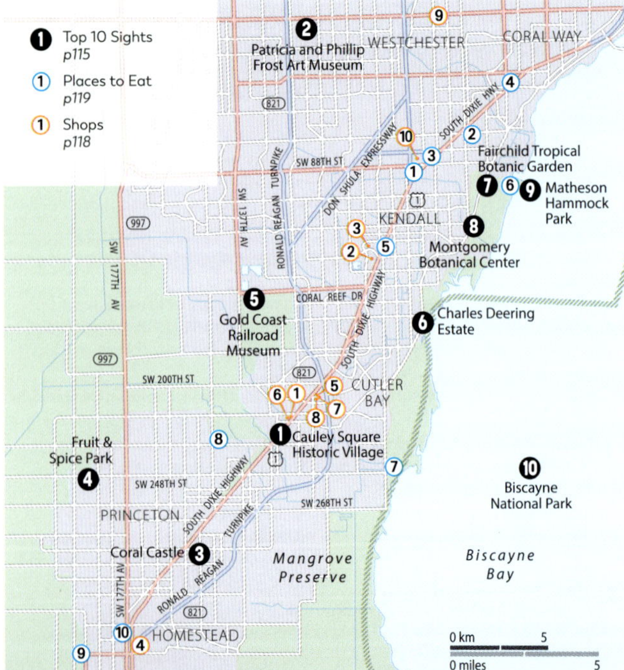

For places to stay in this area, see p151

Edward Leedskalnin's extraordinary Coral Castle

1 Cauley Square Historic Village

E5 22400 Old Dixie Hwy 11am–5pm Tue–Fri, 10am–6pm Sat & Sun cauleysquare.com

This 1903 railroad workers' settlement has been charmingly preserved, with restaurants, art galleries, and stores.

2 Patricia and Phillip Frost Art Museum

F3 10975 SW 17th St 11am–5pm Tue–Sun frost.fiu.edu

Located on the Modesto A. Maidique Campus of the Florida International University (FIU), this museum specializes in Latin American and 20th-century American art, hosting six to eight major exhibitions each year. At the center of the campus is the beautifully landscaped outdoor space, the Avenue of the Arts, which showcases sculpture by well-known artists. Recognized nationally as one of the world's great collections of sculpture –and the largest on a university campus – it includes major pieces by Alexander Liberman, Manuel Mendive, Pablo Atchugarry, and John Henry.

3 Coral Castle

E6 28655 South Dixie Hwy 9am–6pm Thu–Sun coralcastle.com

A castle it isn't, but a conundrum it is. From 1920 to 1940, Latvian immigrant Edward Leedskalnin built this mysterious pile as a valentine to a woman who had jilted him in 1913. No one knows how he single-handedly quarried and transported the 1,100 tons of tough coral rock, carved all the enormous chunks into monumental shapes, and set them all into place so flawlessly. One 9-ton gate is so exquisitely balanced that it opens with the pressure of your little finger.

4 Fruit & Spice Park

E5 24801 Redland Rd (SW 187th Ave), Homestead 305 247 5727 10am–5pm daily

This 37-acre (15-ha) botanical park is home to an impressive variety of tropical plants, including citrus, grape, banana, and bamboo trees, as well as herbs, spices, and nuts. There's also a selection of poisonous species and a store selling unusual fruit products.

5 Gold Coast Railroad Museum

E4 12450 SW 152nd St 11am–4pm Wed–Fri, 10am–4pm Sat & Sun goldcoastrailroadmuseum.org

Founded in 1957 by a group of Miamians who were committed to preserving Florida's rich railroad history, this museum features an excellent collection of artifacts, including the "Ferdinand Magellan," a private railroad car built for President Franklin Roosevelt; the FEC engine that pulled a rescue train from Marathon after the 1935 hurricane; and the 113 locomotive built in 1913. Visitors can also ride on the Edwin Link, a small-gauge children's railroad.

Inside Stone House, Charles Deering Estate

6 Charles Deering Estate

F4 16701 SW 72nd Ave, at SW 167th St & Old Cutler Rd 10am–4pm daily deeringestate.org

Right on Biscayne Bay, this 444-acre (180-ha) estate showcases South Florida's historic architecture and natural beauty. Highlights include Richmond Cottage, built in 1896 as the area's first inn, and the stunning Mediterranean Revival Stone House, dating back to 1922. The grounds are a big attraction, too, with protected mangrove, rockland pine, and tropical hardwood hammock forests. The estate hosts a range of tours and learning programs all year round, including historic ghost tours in the fall. Check the website for details.

7 Fairchild Tropical Botanic Garden

G4 10901 Old Cutler Rd 10am–5pm daily fairchildgarden.org

This immensely beautiful tropical paradise, established in 1938, also serves as a botanical research institute. The garden features lush lowlands and a series of artificial lakes dotted with water lily and lotus plants. Fairchild's collection of cycads – relatives of palms and ferns bearing giant red cones – is one of the world's largest. There's also a butterfly garden, an arboretum, and a small waterfall. For the best panoramas of the garden, walk along the Allée, beginning at the Phillips Courtyard entrance and ending at the terrace of the Overlook. Join a walking tour to learn how plants are used to manufacture everything from Chanel No. 5 to golf balls.

8 Montgomery Botanical Center

G4 11901 Old Cutler Rd montgomerybotanical.org

Formerly a private estate, this 120-acre (48-ha) park was created by Robert and Nell Montgomery, who also founded the Fairchild Botanic Garden. Its aim is to advance the study and conservation of tropical plants, with a focus on palms and cycads from around the world. Note, the center is open for tours only – call 305 667 3800 to pre-book a slot.

HURRICANE COUNTRY

One in ten North Atlantic hurricanes hits Florida – an average of one big storm every two years. In 2018, Hurricane Michael measured Category 5, the worst on the Saffir-Simpson Scale. In 2022, the Category 4 Hurricane Ian became the deadliest storm since 1935, making disastrous landfall in the populated area of Fort Myers on the Gulf Coast.

9 Matheson Hammock Park

G4 9610 Old Cutler Rd
305 665 5475 Sunrise–sunset

Perfect for families, this beachside park famously featured in the 1998 romantic comedy *There's Something About Mary*. It is home to many scenic trails and a unique artificial atoll pool. When you're hungry, head to NOMA Beach at Redfish *(p119)*, set in a 1930s coral rock building.

10 Biscayne National Park

G5 9700 SW 328th St, Homestead nps.gov/bisc

Solitary islands, beautiful coral reefs, sunken shipwrecks, and marine adventures of all manner await at this national park on the edge of the Atlantic. The park is 95 per cent water, therefore most visitors enter it by private boat or book a boat tour via the Biscayne National Park Institute *(biscaynenationalpark institute.org)*. The Dante Fascell Visitor Center *(9am–5pm daily)* at Convoy Point is the only place in the park you can drive to and, from there, you have several boating options. The concession offers canoe rentals, glass-bottom boat tours, snorkel and scuba trips, and transportation to the Elliott and Boca Chita islands for campers. There's also a boardwalk that takes you along the shoreline to the rock jetty beside the boat channel.

Convoy Point boardwalk, Biscayne National Park

DEERING ESTATE WALK

Morning

To get to the **Charles Deering Estate**, drive south from Miami on Highway 1 (Dixie Highway) and turn left on SW 168th Street. Follow it until it dead-ends at the estate on SW 72nd Avenue. A full tour of the grounds will take three to four hours. Follow the Entrance Trail to begin, and as you emerge from the mangroves you will encounter a splendid vista of Biscayne Bay. Note the water-level marker showing the inundation caused by Hurricane Andrew in 1992. Richmond Cottage, the original structure here, was built as an inn in 1896. The Stone House next door contains portraits of the Deering family, and a wine cellar. Head over to the Carriage House, where you can see a vintage gas pump. If you have time, take the Main Nature Trail, which crosses a handsome coral-rock bridge. Finally, walk out through the estate's historic Main Entrance, with its coral-rock pillars, and wood and iron gates.

Afternoon

Picnicking on the grounds is a possibility, and some facilities are provided. Or, for a hearty lunch, take a short drive north to **Guadalajara** *(p119)*. To make a full day's outing, head south along Highway 1 to the eccentric **Coral Castle** *(p115)*.

Shops

Exploring the Falls Shopping Center

1. Twice Vintage

F5 12375 SW 224 St twice-vintage-miami.my shopify.com

Fashionable store with home decor and vintage furniture pieces, as well as clothing and accessories.

2. The Falls Shopping Center

F4 South Dixie Hwy, SW 136th St simon.com/mall/the-falls

This is one of the largest open-air shopping, dining, and entertainment complexes in the country. There are over 100 stores set in a picturesque waterscape with tropical foliage.

3. Art Thyme

F4 8841 SW 132 St artthyme.com

Paint your own pottery or canvas at this studio, which also offers clay modeling, mosaic making, and glass painting. It also sells take-home kits.

4. Metropolis Comics

E6 250 E Palm Dr, Florida City metropoliscomicsmiami.com

Tucked inside the Florida Keys Outlet Marketplace, this little gem offers a wide range of comic books, manga, anime, and video games. It has fresh shipments daily – DC comics arrive on Tuesdays and Marvel on Wednesdays.

5. Survival Miami

F5 20505 South Dixie Hwy, Southland Mall survivalmiami.com

Urban and streetwear brand hailing from south Miami, with a focus on men's sneakers, graphic tees, hoodies, jackets, hats, and bags.

6. Jimmy's Bright Ideas and Antiques

E5 12315 SW 224th St, Goulds 786 208 5853

This lovely cottage store in Cauley Square Historic Village *(p115)* is filled with handcrafted home decor made from re-purposed vintage finds.

7. Southland Mall

F5 20505 South Dixie Hwy mysouthlandmall.com

One of the biggest malls south of Miami houses the likes of Macy's, JC Penney, Old Navy, TJ Maxx, and Victoria's Secret, along with smaller local boutiques.

8. Claire's Boutique

F5 20505 South Dixie Hwy, Southland Mall 305 251 2307

This boutique offers an excellent selection of gift items, from women's earrings and bracelets to hair accessories and purses.

9. Miami Twice

F3 6562 SW 40th St miamitwice.com

Antique-hunters should visit Miami Twice for Art Deco items and other treasures, including vintage designer clothing, handbags, and jewelry from the likes of Chanel, Louis Vuitton, and Gucci.

10. TUMI

G3 7535 N Kendall Dr, Dadeland Mall it.tumi.com

Open since 1975, TUMI offers high-end travel essentials and accessories, including suitcases, backpacks, bags, billfolds, passport cases, and more.

Places to Eat

1. Shorty's BBQ

F4 9200 South Dixie Hwy
305 670 7732 · $$

This South Florida minichain, set up in 1951 by E. L. "Shorty" Allen, is known for its barbecue chicken, pulled pork, and sumptuous baby-back ribs.

PRICE CATEGORIES

For a three-course meal for one with half a bottle of wine (or equivalent meal), taxes, and extra charges.

$ under $35 **$$** $35–$70 **$$$** over $70

2. Whip 'N' Dip Ice Cream

G4 1407 Sunset Dr
whipndip.com · $

Hard-to-resist cakes and ice cream, made with locally sourced ingredients are created on site, with flavors including brownie batter, pumpkin pie, and toasted coconut.

3. Two Chefs

F4 8287 South Dixie Hwy
twochefsrestaurant.com · $$

American and contemporary cuisine with international influences are served in a bistro-style setting.

4. Old Lisbon

F4 5837 Sunset Dr
305 662 7435 · $$

An innovative open-kitchen concept and traditional Portuguese cuisine have made this South Miami restaurant a local favorite since 1991.

5. Guadalajara

F4 8461 SW 132nd St, Pinecrest
guadalajaramiami.com · $

Guadalajara serves hearty portions of home-cooked Mexican fare in a characterful locale. Try dipping a tortilla in the delicious *queso fundido* (cheese fondue).

6. NOMA Beach at Redfish

G4 9610 Old Cutler Rd
noma-beach.com · $$

One of Miami's most romantic spots, NOMA Beach at Redfish is nestled amid the tropical magic of Matheson Hammock Park *(p117)*. Fresh seafood and coastal Italian dishes are prepared by celebrity chef Donatella Arpaia.

7. Black Point Ocean Grill

F5 24775 SW 87th Ave, Cutler Bay
blackpointoceangrill.com · $$

Lively restaurant overlooking Black Point Marina and Black Creek, with a menu of fresh seafood, fish tacos, salads, and sandwiches.

8. Redland Ranch

E5 14655 SW 232nd St
redlandranch.com · $

Tropical produce store with a cult following, offering juices, shakes, smoothies, sandwiches, and fruits.

9. Robert Is Here

E6 19200 SW 344th St, Homestead robertishere.com · $

This legendary fruit stand (now a huge roadside store) has specialized in locally grown rare fruits since 1959. It also serves milkshakes and smoothies.

10. Mi Isla

E6 1380 N Krome Ave, Florida City 786 339 9790 · $

The best place in South Miami to try handmade Cuban desserts, breads, traditional pastries, and a Cuban espresso.

Diners enjoying a meal at Old Lisbon

THE KEYS

The Florida Keys are a string of wild, variegated islands stretching out across the water in a narrow chain. This is an ideal place for various outdoor activities: watersports of all kinds, sportfishing, and hiking through the numerous nature preserves and virgin tropical forests. These islands also have abundant wildlife, including unique flora and fauna, as evidenced by the many parks and family attractions focusing on encounters with nature. Along the only route (US 1, the Overseas Highway) that takes you from the mainland all the way out to Key West, you'll find everything from plush resorts to roadside stands selling wonderful home-grown produce along with fresh seafood.

For places to stay in the area, see p151

1 John Pennekamp Coral Reef State Park

D5 MM 102.5 Key Largo 8am–sunset daily pennekamppark.com

This park is known for its fabulous coral reef life. Visitors can rent canoes, dinghies, or motorboats, as well as snorkeling and scuba gear, or choose a glass-bottom boat ride to explore the waters. Most destinations are actually in the neighboring Florida Keys (Key Largo) National Marine Sanctuary. The shallow waters of Dry Rocks are especially good for snorkeling and scuba diving, as is the nearby Molasses Reef.

Beachgoers relaxing at the Bahia Honda State Park

2 Bahia Honda State Park

B6 36850 Overseas Hwy, Big Pine Key 8am–sunset daily floridastateparks.org/bahiahonda

This protected area has the finest beaches in the Keys – and is voted among the best in the US. Brilliantly white sand is backed by tropical forest crossed by nature trails.

3 Crane Point Hammock Museum and Nature Trails

C6 5550 Overseas Hwy, Marathon 9am–5pm Mon–Sat, noon–5pm Sun cranepoint.net

A 600-year-old dugout canoe, remnants of pirate ships, a simulated coral reef cave, and the Bellarmine jug (c 1580), a shipwreck artifact in almost perfect condition, are on display at this museum. The complex also features a gift shop, and nearby is the colorful Marathon Wild Bird Center.

4 Key West Wildlife Center

A6 1801 White St 11am–2pm Thu–Tue keywestwildlifecenter.org

This wildlife rehabilitation center and nature reserve, located in the 7-acre- (3-ha-) Indigenous Park in Key West, provides refuge for marine and land mammals, wild birds, sea turtles, and tortoises. Wander the pleasant, meandering nature trail.

5 Key West

Rich in breathtaking beauty and in history, the self-styled Conch (pronounced "konk") Republic seems truly a world apart from the rest of the United States *(p40)*.

6 National Key Deer Refuge

B6 30587 Overseas Hwy, Big Pine Key Nature Center: 10am–3pm daily

Spanning a varied landscape of pine forest, mangroves, tropical hardwood hammocks, and fresh- and salt-water wetlands, this refuge is home to 23 endangered and threatened species of flora and fauna, including the Key deer. As a consequence of poaching and loss of habitats, fewer than 50 of these diminutive creatures were left until this refuge was established in 1957. Now there are estimated to be about 600. Drive very slowly and don't feed them.

7 Pigeon Key

B6 1090 Overseas Hwy, Marathon 9:30am–4pm daily pigeonkey.net

This was the site of the work camp for those who built Henry M. Flagler's Overseas Railroad Bridge, described as the eighth wonder of the world when completed in 1912. A marine research foundation has been established in the old buildings. The island is accessible through a ferry service that operates regularly.

8 Florida Keys Wild Bird Rehabilitation Center

C5 92080 Overseas Hwy, Tavernier Sunrise–sunset daily missionwildbird.com

This refuge for native and migratory birds comprises a bird hospital and education center, and a bird sanctuary – 12 acres (5 ha) of wetlands providing a natural habitat for over 120 resident rescued birds, and other flourishing native flora and fauna.

THE KEYS: MYTH AND MAGIC

The very name conjures up visions of windswept seascapes and wild goings-on: Humphrey Bogart and Lauren Bacall in the classic melodrama *Key Largo*; some of the greatest US writers (Ernest Hemingway, Tennessee Williams, et al.) finding their muses where the US meets the Caribbean; and a free, unfettered lifestyle too good to be true.

Gold seal on display, Mel Fisher Maritima Museum

9 Mel Fisher Maritime Museum

A6 200 Greene St, Key West 10am–4pm daily melfisher.org

The maritime museum displays treasure salvaged from shipwrecks from the late 15th to the mid-18th centuries, when Europeans explored what was to them the "New World." Their exploits, their commerce, and their impact on the Indigenous peoples of the Americas can be understood in the artifacts in this museum's collection. Its four ships include the *Nuestra Señora de Atocha*, which sank off Florida in 1622, and the *Henrietta Marie*, an English galleon that sank off the Florida Keys in 1700.

10 Indian Key Historic State Park

C5 Offshore Island, Islamorada 8am–sunset daily floridastate parks.org/indiankey

Tiny Indian Key has a surprisingly large amount of history for its size (10.5 acres/4.25 ha). An ancient Native American site, it was settled in 1831 by Captain J. Houseman, an opportunistic wrecker. In 1840, Seminoles attacked, killing the settlers. The Key was abandoned, and today only the outlines of the village remain, overgrown by vegetation. These are the descendants of plants belonging to Dr. Henry Perrine, a botanist who was killed in the raid.

Pigeon Key, beneath the Seven Mile Bridge

A DAY'S WALK ON KEY WEST

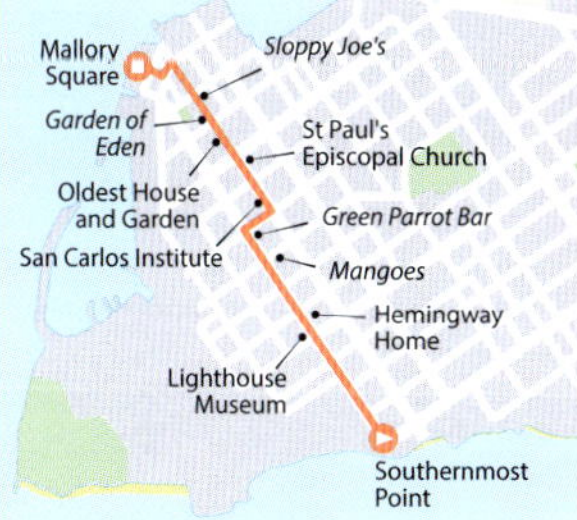

Morning

Start at the **Southernmost Point** in the continental US, overlooking the Atlantic at the intersection of Whitehead and South streets. Then head up Whitehead to the **Lighthouse Museum** *(p41)* and climb its 88 steps for a great overview of the island and beyond. Next stop is the **Hemingway Home** *(p40)*, at No. 907; here you can take a trip through the writer's life as a Conch. Then move on to the **Green Parrot Bar** *(p130)*, at No. 601 Whitehead, to admire its funkiness and have a drink before lunch. From here, head over to Duval Street, to **Mangoes** restaurant *(p131)* at No. 700, for a great lunch and people-watching.

Afternoon

Admire the Spanish Colonial facade of the **San Carlos Institute**, and the stained-glass windows of **St. Paul's Episcopal Church**. At No. 322, visit the **Oldest House Museum and Garden** *(305 294 9502)*. Now things might get very "Key West," as you climb to the third floor of the **Bull and Whistle Bar** *(p130)* to find the **Garden of Eden** *(p63)*, a clothing-optional bar where no cameras or cell phones are allowed. Farther along stop at **Sloppy Joe's** *(p130)*. By now, it should be time for the sunset celebration, so head down to **Mallory Square** *(p40)*.

Nature Preserves

Alligator at the Crocodile Lake Wildlife Refuge

1. Crocodile Lake Wildlife Refuge

D5 10750 County Rd 905, Key Largo 305 451 4223 Sunrise–sunset daily

Part of the United States National Wildlife Refuge System, this sanctuary for endangered American crocodiles is closed to the public, but there is an information kiosk and a public garden.

2. Key Largo Hammock Botanical State Park

D5 Country Rd 905, MM 106 floridastateparks.org Sunrise–sunset daily

The largest remaining tropical West Indian hardwood and mangrove hammock is a refuge for protected indigenous flora and fauna.

3. Great White Heron Reserve

C5 30587 Overseas Hwy, Long Key 305 872 0774 8am–sunset daily

This refuge was founded as a haven for herons and various migratory birds.

4. Green Turtle Hammock

C5 30587 Overseas Hwy, Long Key 305 853 1685 8am–sunset daily

A small thicket of tropical foliage, this is a great place to spot crocodiles.

5. Dagny Johnson Key Largo Hammock Botanical State Park

C5 905 County Road, Key Largo floridastateparks.org 8am–sunset daily

Located in the center of Key Largo, this tropical park offers a network of shaded walking trails.

6. Windley Key Fossil Reef State Geological Park

C5 84900 Overseas Hwy, Islamorada 305 664 2540 8am–5pm Thu–Mon

There are nature displays in the center of the park and trails lead into the railroad's old quarries, where you can see fossilized brain coral and sea ferns.

7. Lignumvitae Key Botanical State Park

C5 77200 Overseas Hwy, Islamorada floridastateparks.org Park: 8am–4pm Thu–Mon; ferry: 1–4pm Fri–Sun

This beautiful virgin hardwood forest, along with its historic home and gardens, built by William Matheson, is accessible only by boat.

8. Long Key State Park

C6 67400 Overseas Hwy, Long Key floridastateparks.org 8am–sunset daily

The boardwalk at Long Key cuts through a biodiverse mangrove swamp.

9. Bahia Honda State Park

Heavily forested and with great nature trails, this park *(p121)* offers sublime snorkeling experiences.

10. Looe Key National Marine Sanctuary

B6 MM 27.5 oceanside 305 872 3210

One of the Keys' most spectacular coral reefs, Looe Key is great for snorkeling and diving. Call for boat trips to the best spots.

Plants and Animals

1. Coral
Although it appears to be an insensate rock, coral is actually a living organism of various species, very fragile and easily damaged by the slightest touch.

2. Palms
Although only a few species of palm are natives in the Keys – the royal palm, the sabal palm, the saw palmetto, and the thatch palm – a huge range of imported palms now adorn the islands.

3. Egrets
Often visible on the islands, and similar to herons, are the great egret, the snowy egret (distinguishable by its black legs and yellow feet), and the reddish egret.

4. Double-Crested Cormorant
Notable for its S-curved neck, distinctive hooked beak, and spectacular diving skills, this is one of the most fascinating of Keys birds.

5. White Ibis
Recognizable by its long, down-curving beak, this medium-sized white wading bird, numerous in Florida, was sacred to the Egyptians.

6. Sea Turtles
These long-lived creatures come in a wide variety of shapes and sizes. From the largest to the smallest they are the leatherback, the loggerhead, the green, the hawksbill, and the Ridley turtles.

7. Herons
These elegant long-legged birds include the great blue heron, the white phase heron, the little blue heron, the tricolored heron, the green-backed heron, and the black-crowned night heron.

8. Gumbo Limbo Tree
Called the "tourist tree" due to its red and peeling bark which resembles sunburnt skin, this unmistakable species – a Florida native – is found all over the Keys.

9. Key Deer
The diminutive Key deer are found primarily on Big Pine and No Name keys. These tiny, docile creatures reach a maximum height of about 30 in (80 cm).

10. Threatened and Endangered Species
The Florida Keys conceal many endangered species. These include the American crocodile, Schaus swallowtail butterfly, Key Largo wood rat and cotton mouse, and roseate spoonbill, all of which have either been hunted near to the point of extinction or lost their habitats due to human encroachment.

Key deer crossing a swamp, Big Pine

Exploring the vibrant coral reefs off Key Largo

Outdoor Activities

1. Swimming
Some of the best beaches in the world are in the Keys. Don't worry if the ocean temperature falls below the usual 79° F (26° C), as most hotels have heated swimming pools.

2. Fishing
The Keys are a paradise for deep-sea fishing. With the Gulf Stream nearby, these waters offer the most varied fishing imaginable. Boat trips are easy to come by – Good Times Key West *(goodtimeskeywest.com)* is a top choice for both solo and group trips.

3. Water-Skiing and Jet-Skiing
Water-skiing and jet-skiing are available wherever there's a marina, especially in developed tourist areas. Sunset Watersports *(sunsetwatersportskeywest.com)* is one of the operators offering jet-ski tours in the Keys.

4. Boating and Sailing
The Keys are home to dozens of marinas, where tour operators offer a variety of boat rentals. Private boating and sailing expeditions can also be arranged for larger groups.

5. Cycling
There is no doubt that cycling is one of the best ways to see the Keys. The roads are fairly bike-friendly, especially in Key West, and bicycle rentals are readily available.

6. Tennis
Good tennis clubs can be found on just about every popular Key – on Islamorada at MM 76.8 bayside, Marathon at MM 53.5 oceanside, on Key West, of course, and elsewhere.

7. Golf
The Keys don't have as many golf courses as the rest of Florida, but there are several good ones, such as Key Colony Beach Golf, near Marathon, and Key West Golf Club, which is a more premium option for avid golf players.

8. Parasailing
As close to growing wings as you can get, parasailing is an easy, safe, and unforgettable adventure. Several tour operators, such as Sebago *(keywestsebago.com)*, offer this thrilling experience.

9. Windsurfing
With prevailing winds and shallow waters that remain so for miles out to sea, the Keys are ideal for windsurfing. Most busy beaches up and down the islands have shops that rent the necessary equipment.

10. Snorkeling and Scuba Diving
The Keys are almost entirely surrounded by America's largest living coral reef and the underwater world is one of the main treats for visitors and locals alike.

Special Tours and Events

1. Dry Tortugas

A paradisical, undeveloped collection of islands *(p133)*, where the snorkeling is unbeatable. Key West Seaplane Adventure *(keywestseaplanecharters.com)* offer various tour options and packages.

2. Key West Ghost Hunt

301 Whitehead St, Key West
ghosthuntkeywest.com

Discover the supernatural with a 90-minute stroll through the mysterious streets of Key West's Old Town. Tours depart every evening from the First Flight Restaurant and Bar.

3. Seven-Mile Bridge Run

Marathon Key Late Mar–mid-Apr 7mbrun.com

Enthusiastic runners take on the Seven-Mile Bridge in this race, which has been held every year since 1982 and raises money for various Marathon charities.

4. Bahama Village Goombay Festival

Bahama Village, Key West

This festival is a celebration of vibrant Island culture and life. Held in mid-October, it usually merges with the Fantasy Fest.

5. Key West Fantasy Fest

Last 2 weeks of Oct
fantasyfest.com

Revelers throng the streets in outlandish costumes during this ten-day festival. Popular events include street fairs, parades and glamorous balls *(p79)*.

6. Old Town Trolley Tour in Key West

trolleytours.com/key-west

Jump aboard this orange and green trolley to see the sights of Key West. A ticket for the narrated tour allows you to hop on and off all day.

7. Hemingway Days

Held in the middle of the low season, during the third week of July (Ernest Hemingway's birthday was July 21st), this party is most loved by the locals, or "Conchs", who attend in great numbers . Hemingway look-alikes lead the celebrations and tributes to the famous writer.

8. Annual Conch-Blowing Contest

This traditional means of musical expression – or noise-making in less-skilled cases – fills the air over Key West in early March, when visitors and locals alike come to showcase their conch-blowing skills.

9. New Year's Eve in Key West

In Key West, welcoming the New Year starts with the Last Sunset celebration at Mallory Square, followed by several exciting local acts and fireworks on Blackwater Sound.

10. Conch Tour Train

303 Front St, Key West
conchtourtrain.com

Key West's train tour is a must-do for first-time visitors. It gives an overview of the place and all sorts of insights into its history and culture.

The Conch Tour Train outside Sloppy Joe's

Island Shopping

African wood carvings on sale, Archeo

1. Archeo

A6 1208 Duval St, Key West
archeogallery.com

Shop for African masks, wood carvings, and stunning Persian rugs at this chic gallery.

2. The Gallery at Kona Kai Resort

C5 MM 97.8 bayside, 97802 Overseas Hwy konakairesort.com

This gallery showcases an impressive collection of international artwork, including several paintings by Sobran and Magni, powerful bronze sculptures, and fine Keys nature photography.

3. The Shops at Mallory Square

A6 291 Front St, Key West

This 19th-century US Navy coal depot was converted into a two-level shopping center. It is now home to local artisans, jewelry-makers, and several gift and souvenir stores.

4. Bésame Mucho

A6 315 Petronia St, Key West
besamemucho.net

This boutique, in the Bahama Village neighborhood, sells lovely gifts such as candles, jewelry, and home decor.

5. Kino Sandals

A6 107 Fitzpatrick St, Key West
kinosandals.com

This sandal factory produces original designs, each pair carefully handmade by artisans using natural leather uppers and natural rubber soles.

6. Kermit's Key West Key Lime Shoppe

A6 200 Elizabeth St, Key West
keylimeshop.com

This pretty little shop serves one of the tastiest key lime pies in town, along with key lime-flavor cookies, salsa, chutney, taffy, tea, and olive oil.

7. Key West Aloe

A6 416 Greene St, Key West
keywestaloe.com

A company that has made its own all-natural products since 1971, without any animal testing.

8. Tucker's Provisions

A6 611 Duval St, Key West
tuckersprovisions.com

Set in the center of Duval, this popular store is packed with all sorts of gifts and souvenir pieces that are unique to the Key West, including hats, traditional clothing, bags, wallets, and other accessories.

9. Old Road Gallery

C5 88888 Old Hwy, Tavernier
oldroadgallery.com

Peruse lovely beach-themed artworks crafted by local artists at this pleasant gallery. There's also an on-site sculpture garden and pottery studio.

10. Grand Vin

A6 1107 Duval St, Key West

If you are looking for excellent wines from around the world at reasonable prices, and the chance to sample many by the glass – this is the place to visit. Sit out on the porch with your wine and enjoy the view.

LGBTQ+ Venues

1. Bobby's Monkey Bar
A6 900 Simonton St, Key West
305 294 2655
Lively gay bar popular with both locals and visitors thanks to its friendly staff and offbeat events.

2. Saloon 1
A6 504 Petronia St, Key West
9pm–4am daily
Bawdy gay leather bar with a seductive atmosphere and friendly bartenders.

3. La-Te-Da
A6 1125 Duval St, Key West
305 296 6706
This upscale venue with a restaurant is a popular LGBTQ+ spot. "Guys as Dolls" and other acts are performed in the Crystal Room Cabaret nightly.

4. Graffiti
A6 721 Duval St, Key West
305 295 0003
Expect trendy fashion pieces that perfectly capture the vibe of the island.

5. Bourbon Street Complex
A6 722–801 Duval St, Key West
Included here are the Bourbon Street Pub, the 801 Bourbon Bar, Saloon 1, Pizza Joe's, and the New Orleans House. The 801 also features nightly drag shows.

6. Gay Key West Visitor Center
A6 808 Duval St, Key West
gaykeywestfl.com
There's always plenty of information here for the taking, as well as occasional meetings and social events.

7. Aqua Night Club
A6 711 Duval St, Key West
305 916 1255
This vibrant club hosts a karaoke and drag show. The poolside bar out back is quieter, with torches and a waterfall. Happy hour from noon to 6pm.

8. The Mermaid & The Alligator
A6 729 Truman Ave, Key West
kwmermaid.com
With lush gardens and posh amenities, this elegant bed-and-breakfast is a great LGBTQ+-friendly option.

9. Santa Maria Suites
A6 1401 Simonton St, Key West
305 296 5678
Located 3 miles (4.8 km) from the airport and 8 minutes from the beach, this classy resort is popular with LGBTQ+ travelers.

10. Island House Key West
A6 Atlantic Ocean end of White St Pier
This popular gay resort features a palm-fringed pool, 24-hour poolside bar, and a jacuzzi where clothing is optional.

Colorful drag show at Bourbon Street Complex

Bars, Pubs, and Clubs

1. Captain Tony's Saloon

A6 428 Greene St

This was the original Sloppy Joe's, where Hemingway was a regular. Live bands feature regularly and Conch legend Jimmy Buffett used to sing here.

2. Sloppy Joe's

A6 201 Duval St 305 294 5717

Grab a meal or a drink at this lively bar. It's heavy on Hemingway memorabilia, since he used to hang out here as well as at the original Sloppy Joe's.

3. Green Parrot Bar

A6 601 Whitehead St
305 294 6133

Established in 1890, the Green Parrot Bar is a favorite among locals and offers live music shows on the weekends.

4. Bull and Whistle Bar

A6 224 Duval St 305 296 4545

The Bull and Whistle Bar features three bars, each on a different floor. The street-level bar buzzes with live entertainment, while the top-floor deck houses the famous clothing-optional bar, Garden of Eden *(p63)*.

Facade of the Bull and Whistle Bar

5. Jimmy Buffett's Margaritaville

A6 500 Duval St 305 292 1435

Local-boy-made-good Jimmy Buffett is the owner of this bar-restaurant-souvenir shop. There is nightly live music, and on occasion the Parrot Head leader himself shows up.

6. Little Room Jazz Club

A6 821 Duval St 305 741 7515

Tune into some jazz while sipping delicious island cocktails at this popular spot for music lovers. Gourmet grub pub, wine, and craft beers are also offered here.

7. Schooner Wharf Bar

A6 202 William St 305 292 9520

Located in the Historic Seaport District, this bar offers open-air views of the waterfront along with live music performances.

8. Hog's Breath Saloon

A6 400 Front St 305 296 4222

One of the best-known bars in Key West, Hog's Breath was founded in 1988. Visitors can expect a traditional saloon bar setting, lots of heavy drinking, and live music.

9. The Rum Bar

A6 1117 Duval St 305 296 2680

Housed in the Speakeasy Inn, this bar offers excellent island cocktails and a wraparound porch, where you can enjoy lovely views and great people-watching.

10. Rick's Bar/Durty Harry's Entertainment Complex

A6 202 Duval St 305 296 4890

This large complex has eight separate bars, with Rick's Bar, located on the top floor – being one of the hottest dance clubs in town.

Outdoor seating area at Blue Heaven

Places to Eat

PRICE CATEGORIES

For a three-course meal for one with half a bottle of wine (or equivalent meal), taxes, and extra charges.

$ under $35 $$ $35–$70 $$$ over $70

1. Blue Heaven

A6 729 Thomas St 305 296 8666 · $$

Trademark Key West chickens and cats wander about in the garden of this wonderful Caribbean restaurant.

2. Tavern N Town

A6 3841 N Roosevelt Blvd 305 296 8100 · $$$

Sample Floribbean cuisine in the elegant surroundings of this restaurant. The conch chowder is a must-try.

3. A & B Lobster House

A6 700 Front St 305 294 5880 · $$$

Enjoy Maine lobster, fresh shrimp, and waterfront views at this historic spot.

4. Mangoes

A6 700 Duval St 305 294 8002 · $$

Mangoes is known for its delicious fare – its Key West Loaded Pineapple Salad is a house specialty.

5. Louie's Backyard

A6 700 Waddell Ave 305 294 1061 · $$$

Enticing haute cuisine in an easy, breezy setting right on the Atlantic.

6. Mangia Mangia Pasta Café

A6 900 Southard St 305 294 2469 · $$

Open only for dinner, this central Italian café has superb fresh pasta dishes.

7. Conch Republic Seafood Company

A6 631 Greene St 305 294 4403 · $$

Tuck into fresh seafood prepared in the traditional Conch style at this venue, which also hosts private parties.

8. Sarabeth's

A6 530 Simonton St at Southard 305 293 8181 · $$

The fluffy omelets, key lime pie French toast, and lemon ricotta pancakes make this a favorite for Sunday brunch.

9. El Siboney

A6 900 Catherine St 305 296 4184 · $

Try a variety of dishes here, such as roast pork with cassava and tamale, or breaded *palomilla* steak.

10. One Duval

A6 Pier House Resort, 1 Duval St 305 2953255 · $$

One Duval focuses on using spices and ingredients indigenous to the Caribbean and Florida peninsula to prepare innovative dishes that redefine the regional cuisine.

SIDE TRIPS

Prepare to swap city crowds for biodiverse islands and shopping malls for historic forts as you venture out of the busier confines of Greater Miami. North of the city, the Gold and Treasure Coasts are a much-loved destination for both vacationers and retirees, with their sun-kissed beaches and seaside resorts. The region of the Gulf Coast is rich with both city pleasures and spectacular nature. Most visitors head for the chic resorts of Sanibel and Captiva islands, but the remote beauty of less developed islands is equally appealing. The vast swamps and wild waters of the Everglades act as a fascinating natural contrast to the beach- and city-focused tourism in the rest of the state, making for an ideal excursion in southern Florida.

For places to stay in the area, see p137

Luxury homes by the water, Fort Myers

1 Fort Myers

A2

Famous as the base of operations for the 19th-century inventor Thomas Alva Edison, Fort Myers is home to the Edison & Ford Winter Estates, which commemorates Edison and the motor car mogul Henry Ford. Other attractions include the family-friendly IMAG History & Science Center, the Caloosahatchee River, and Fort Myer's historic downtown. To the southwest, on Estero Island, is the Fort Myers Beach, known for its miles of sandy stretches.

2 Sanibel and Captiva Islands

A3

The Lee Island Coast has irresistible sandy beaches, rare wildlife, lush vegetation, and wonderful sunsets. The jewels in the crown are the Sanibel and Captiva Islands, which have a Caribbean-style laid-back vibe mixed with upscale shops and restaurants. Much of the territory is protected, and development limited: there are a few high-rise hotels, and mainly just houses and cottages.

3 Dry Tortugas from Key West

A5

Travel to the wonderful islands of the Dry Tortugas by seaplane or ferry from Key West *(p127)*. The Yankee Freedom ferry company *(800634 0939)* offers a daily trip. The day-long tours include food and snorkeling gear. Camping overnight is also possible. The most visited island is Garden Key, the site of Fort Jefferson and its fantastic snorkeling beaches *(p59)*.

4 Loxahatchee National Wildlife Refuge

D3 10216 Lee Rd, Boynton Beach 561 734 8303 Hours vary, call ahead

This is the only surviving remnant of the northern Everglades, a vast area of mostly sawgrass marsh that is so characteristic of the Everglades environment. The inviting public-use areas provide viewing opportunities for a large variety of wetland flora and fauna, including egrets, alligators, and the endangered snail kite. Activities include nature walks, hiking, canoeing, birdwatching, and bass-fishing. A 5-mile (8-km) canoe trail provides the best way to see and explore the refuge up close.

5 A1A North along the Treasure Coast

D2

If you continue on the A1A north of Palm Beach, the megalopolis gives way to the quieter towns of the Treasure Coast. These include Vero, the largest; Stuart, with its charming historic district; Fort Pierce; and, at the northern extension of the Treasure Coast, the fishing village of Sebastian.

Aquatic plants, Big Cypress Seminole Reservation

6 Big Cypress Seminole Reservation

B3–C3

Located on the northern border of the Big Cypress National Preserve, the largest Seminole reservation in the state of Florida is the best place to meet the locals and get some sense of the lives of the modern tribe. The main Seminole settlement can be found 15 miles (24 km) north of the I-75, and has a few basic diners and gift shops, as well as the illuminating Ah-Tah-Thi-Ki Museum *(p48)*, where videos, a rare collection of clothing and artifacts, and exhibitions by Seminole artists highlight the history and cultural traditions of the tribe.

7 The Everglades, across the Tamiami Trail (Highway 41)

A3–C4

Highway 41 was the first cut across the Everglades and from its inception has been called the Tamiami Trail, which stands for Tampa-Miami, the two cities it connects. However, it does take you into Seminole country, where you can experience the wonders of the Everglades *(p42)*. As you head to the Gulf Coast, stop at Everglades City and Naples.

Pier stretching over the waters at Naples

8 A1A North along the Gold Coast

Starting just at the northern tip of Miami Beach is a vast stretch of beautiful, wealthy communities that goes on for at least 50 miles (80 km). As diverse in their own ways as the Greater Miami area, they add immeasurably to the cultural richness of South Florida, and most offer large, enticing swathes of sand *(p38)*. Along the route, visitors can explore fascinating museums, parks, nature centers and monuments, along with breathtaking beaches and swimming spots.

HURRICANE SEASON

Hurricane Ian made landfall in September 2022, causing mass destruction across Florida and western Cuba. Buildings and infrastructure on Sanibel Island and the islands off Fort Myers were badly damaged. The Atlantic hurricane season brought 18 named storms and 11 hurricanes, resulting in extensive damage across Florida.

9 The Everglades, across Alligator Alley (I-75)

B3–C3

This toll road across the Everglades keeps you at arm's length from the swampy, teeming mass. Along the way you will find several great stops, including restaurants, dive bars, and sunset points, as you pass through Big Cypress National Preserve and north of Fakahatchee Strand State Preserve *(p43)*.

10 Naples and Around

A3

If you cross the Everglades, your inevitable first stop on the Gulf Coast will be Naples. An affluent beach city, Naples prides itself on its manicured appearance, 90 golf courses, and an elegant downtown area. There's a pleasant pier where you can commune with pelicans or do some fishing, and 10 miles (16 km) of pristine, sugary beaches, with warmer waters than the Atlantic Ocean. Nearby Marco Island, the most northerly of the Ten Thousand Islands archipelago, is a good base for delving into the western fringe of the Everglades. It has been the source of significant Calusa finds, some dating back 3,500 years.

A DAY TRIP ALONG THE A1A NORTH OF FORT LAUDERDALE

Morning

Drive north along Highway A1A to ritzy **Boca Raton**, one of South Florida's wealthiest communities and sprinkled with 1920s Mediterranean Revival architecture by Addison Mizner. Stop at the **Gumbo Limbo Nature Center** *(p38)*, and look for ospreys, brown pelicans, and the occasional manatee. Pop across to adjacent **Red Reef Park** *(p58)* for sunbathing and swimming. Retrace your route back to the Palmetto Park Road junction and turn right – a block on the right is local favorite **Boca Beach House** *(887 E Palmetto Park Rd)*.

Afternoon

Continue 9 miles (14 km) north on Highway A1A to the **Sandoway Discovery Center**. In this 1936 beachfront house, exhibits include a butterfly garden, shell gallery, and coral reef pool with live sharks. Drive 9 miles (14 km) north before taking a left at Ocean Avenue for a pit stop at the **Old Key Lime House** *(p61)* in Lantana, a 19th-century throwback with great key lime pies. End the day with a final 9 miles (14 km) along the A1A to **Palm Beach** *(p60)*. Take in the plush shops along **Worth Avenue** *(p75)*, before cocktails at the opulent **Breakers** *(p150)*.

Wooden lodge and grounds, Rod and Gun Club

Places to Eat

1. Rod and Gun Club
B4 200 W Broadway, Everglades City 239 695 2101 · $$
Housed in a classic Florida frontier hotel, Rod and Gun Club offers fresh fish sandwiches and great views.

2. Okeechobee Steakhouse
D2 2854 Okeechobee Blvd, West Palm Beach 561 683 5151 · $$$
This old-fashioned steakhouse, open since 1947, serves juicy rib eye and porterhouse steaks.

3. The Veranda
A2 2122 2nd St, Fort Myers 239 332 2065 · $$$
A charming restaurant, with Deep South decor, The Veranda offers a menu featuring blue crab cakes, steaks, and salads.

4. Swamp Water Café
C2 30000 Gator Tail Trail 863 983 6101 · $
The menu at this café features classic traditional American dishes and various Indigenous American delicacies. Try the Indian taco or fry bread with honey butter.

5. Joanie's Blue Crab Café
B4 39395 Tamiami Trail E, Ochopee 239 695 2682 · $
This old-fashioned seafood shack on the edge of the Everglades offers a no-frills dining experience. Open for lunch most days, this spot serves fresh seafood.

PRICE CATEGORIES

For a three-course meal for one with half a bottle of wine (or equivalent meal), taxes, and extra charges.

$ under $35 $$ $35–$70 $$$ over $70

6. HaVannA Cafe
B4 191 Smallwood Dr, Chokoloskee 239 695 2214 · $$
Located on Chokoloskee Island, this hidden gem combines classic Cuban cooking with fresh seafood.

7. Sinclair's Ocean Grill
D2 Jupiter Beach Resort, 5 North A1A 561 745 7120 · $$$
Sample traditional Floribbean food and tasty cocktails at this cozy café.

8. The Dock at Crayton Cove
A3 845 12th Ave S at Naples Bay 239 263 9940 · $$$
Head to The Dock to try the macadamia nut-crusted snapper and delicious key lime grouper.

9. Keylime Bistro
A3 11509 Andy Rosse Lane, Captiva Island 239 395 4000 · $$
The tricolor vegetarian terrine is a must-try at this trendy bistro.

10. MudBugs Cajun Kitchen
A3 1473 Periwinkle Way, Sanibel Island mudbugssanibel.com · $$
Enjoy a slice of the bayou on Sanibel, with live music and Cajun cuisine.

Places to Stay

PRICE CATEGORIES

For a standard double room per night (with breakfast if included), taxes, and extra charges.

$ under $200 $$ $200–$400
$$$ over $400

1. Trail Lakes
B4 40904 Tamiami Trail, Hwy 41, Ochopee evergladescamping.net · $$
There are camping sites, cabins, and thatched-roof chickee huts. Amenities are extremely basic but allow you to experience the Everglades up close.

2. Rod and Gun Lodge
B4 200 W Broadway, Everglades City rodandguneverglades.com · $
This lodge has hosted iconic guests, including Hemingway, US presidents, and Mick Jagger.

3. Conrad Fort Lauderdale
D3 551 N Fort Lauderdale Beach Blvd 954 414 5100 · $$$
The nautical-style decor of this hotel is second only to its oceanfront location. It offers superb views, an elevated pool, and a tranquil spa.

4. Casa Grandview
D2 1410 Georgia Ave, West Palm Beach casagrandview.com · $$
Set in the historic Grandview Heights district, this luxurious B&B offers romantic suites and a buffet breakfast served on its beautiful veranda.

5. Jupiter Beach Resort
D2 5 North A1A, Jupiter jupiterbeachresort.com · $$
The rooms at this resort have stunning marble baths, colorful furnishings, and terrific waterfront views.

6. Marriott Sanibel Harbour Resort and Spa
A3 17260 Harbour Pointe Dr, Fort Myers marriott.com · $$
Spacious and light rooms, and a recreational area with a private beach.

7. Island Inn
A3 3111 W Gulf Dr, Sanibel Island islandinnsanibel.com · $$$
Luxury inn that survived and rebuilt quickly after Hurricane Ian in 2022, with boutique studios and suites that have balconies overlooking the beach.

8. Waterstone Resort & Marina
D3 999 E Camino Real, Boca Raton waterstoneboca.com · $$$
On the shores of Lake Boca, this plush hotel offers easy access to watersports and waterside dining.

9. Clewiston Inn
C2 108 Royal Palm Ave, Clewiston 863 301 3752 · $
This charming inn evokes the atmosphere of a pre-Civil War era with its carefully curated decor.

10. Inn on Fifth
A3 699 5th Ave S, Naples innonfifth.com · $$
With its Mediterranean charm, elegant courtyards, lavish fountains, and cozy rooms, Inn on Fifth is the perfect spot for a relaxing stay.

Luxurious suite at the Inn on Fifth

STREETSMART

Miami Metrorail from above

GETTING AROUND

Whether you are visiting for a short Miami city break or a relaxed island-hopping holiday in the Keys, discover how best to reach your destination and travel like a pro.

AT A GLANCE

PUBLIC TRANSPORT COSTS

MIAMI
$2.25
Single Ticket Metrorail

MIAMI-DADE COUNTY
$5.00
EASY Ticket Day Pass

MIAMI TO KEY WEST
$25
Single Shuttle Ticket

SPEED LIMITS

NEAR SCHOOLS	RESIDENTIAL AREAS
20 mph (30 km/h)	**30 mph** (50 km/h)

RURAL ROADS	FREEWAYS
50 mph (85 km/h)	**70 mph** (110 km/h)

Arriving by Air

Most major international airlines serve **Miami International Airport**. The free MIA Mover links the airport with the Miami Intermodal Center, comprising the Rental Car Center and Miami Central Station (with bus and Metrorail services).

Fort Lauderdale-Hollywood International Airport is the region's second airport. Broward County Transit bus No. 1 provides a cheap service to Fort Lauderdale, and there are free shuttles to the nearest Tri-Rail station at Dania Beach.

Key West International Airport serves only a handful of US destinations.

Fort Lauderdale-Hollywood International Airport
W broward.org
Key West International Airport
W eyw.com
Miami International Airport
W miami-airport.com

Arriving by Sea

The **Port of Miami** is the busiest cruise ship hub in the world. It is accessible by car or taxi, though most cruise lines offer direct shuttle services to Miami International Airport.

Port of Miami
W miamidade.gov/portmiami

Train Travel

Amtrak, the national passenger rail company, serves Florida from the east coast. There is one daily service from New York City. This Silver Service takes up to 28 hours, and runs via Washington D.C., down through Jacksonville and Orlando, terminating in Miami. Sleepers and meals are available on this journey. The Palmetto serves the same route and offers a business-class service.

If you want to travel by train to Florida but take your own car to drive once you get there, book a ticket on

Amtrak's Auto Train, which runs daily from Lorton in Virginia to Sanford, Florida – 250 miles (400 km) north of Miami. The journey takes about 18 hours.

Amtrak also offers local train services around south Florida. Trains stop at several stations between Fort Lauderdale, West Palm Beach, and Miami Central Station.

If you are planning to make more than a couple of trips by train, it is worth buying a rail pass, which gives unlimited travel on Amtrak's network during a set period of time. The pass must be bought before you arrive – either online with Amtrak or through a verified travel agent that deals with Amtrak.

Amtrak
W amtrak.com

Long-distance Bus Travel

Whether you are traveling from other parts of the country or within Florida, **Greyhound** buses offer the cheapest way to get around. There is a good, although fairly slow, service between Miami Central Station and Key West, as well as buses to Fort Lauderdale, West Palm Beach, and most coastal towns in between.

Passes provide unlimited travel for set periods of time (between four and 60 days), but you may only find them particularly useful if you have a very full itinerary. Overseas visitors should also note that passes often cost less if bought from a Greyhound agent outside the US.

Greyhound
W greyhound.com

Public Transportation

Miami has the **Metrobus, Metrorail**, and **Metromover.** Metrorail is a 25-mile (40-km) rail line. It provides a useful link between the most popular tourist areas of Coral Gables, Coconut Grove, the Downtown area, and Miami airport. Services run daily every 10 minutes or so from 5am until midnight.

Metromover is Miami's free monorail. It has three loops, connecting the heart of Downtown with the Omni entertainment and Brickell financial districts on separate elevated lines. There are 21 stations in total.

The free **Miami Beach Trolley** offers four popular routes running every 20 minutes 8am to 11pm daily. Routes include North Beach to Normandy Isle, 41st Street to Collins Avenue (Middle Beach loop), and the South Beach Trolley loop – with stops between 5th Street and Lincoln Road. The Collins Express trolley route links the Middle Beach and North Beach trolleys.

Metrobus, Metromover and Metrorail
W miamidade.gov/transit
Miami Beach Trolley
W miamibeachfl.gov/cityhall/transportation/trolley

Tickets

You can get an EASY Ticket as a paper card or via the GO Miami-Dade Transit app. It can be loaded with top-up money and 1- and 7-Day Passes. Bus drivers also accept payments in cash using exact change, though fewer passengers now pay with cash. There are often discounted passes for multiple trips as well as reduced rates for children.

JOURNEY DISTANCES IN SOUTH FLORIDA

Start	Destination	Distance	Public Transport
Miami Airport	Miami Beach	10 miles (16 km)	$3.25
Orlando Airport	Miami Beach	240 miles (390 km)	$60-70
Miami Beach	Fort Lauderdale	30 miles (50 km)	$20
Fort Lauderdale	Key West	190 miles (310 km)	$40
Miami Beach	Everglades	30 miles (50 km)	$10

Taxis

Taxis are a comfortable though expensive way of getting around. Cabs can be picked up at taxi ranks and hotels in larger city centers, as well as at airports. Most have a "TAXI" sign on the roof; this is illuminated if the taxi is free. They can also be booked by telephone or online. **Yellow Cab Taxis**, which operate in Miami, start at $2.95 for the first sixth of a mile, and $0.85 for each additional sixth of a mile until 1 mile. Then it's $0.55 per additional sixth of a mile. Ride-hailing apps also operate in the city.

Yellow Cab Taxis
W yellowtaximiami.com

Water Taxis

In Miami and Fort Lauderdale, local **Water Taxis** are a fun way to explore the area's 300 miles (482 km) of canals. Routes are generally geared to tourists, and as a result they are fairly limited in scope – linking hotels, restaurants, and stores, for example. However, it's great for sightseeing and you'll often find special fares.

Fort Lauderdale Water Taxi
W watertaxi.com
Miami Water Taxi
W watertaximiami.com

Car Rental

Rental car companies are based at airports and other locations in major towns and cities. It is usually cheaper to rent a vehicle at the airport rather than from a downtown outlet.

All you need to rent a car is your driver's license, passport, and a credit card. If you present a debit card, you may have to pay a larger deposit. The minimum age for car rental is 21, but drivers under 25 may need to pay a surcharge.

The state of Florida requires that you carry a copy of the rental agreement in the car. It is recommended to store it safely out of sight.

Make sure your car rental agreement includes Collision Damage Waiver (CDW) – also known as Loss Damage Waiver (LDW) – or you'll be liable for any damage to the car, even if it was not your fault. Rental agreements include third-party insurance, but this is rarely adequate. It is advisable to buy additional or supplementary liability insurance, just in case.

Most companies add a premium if you want to drop the car off in another city, and all impose high charges for gas: if you return the car with less fuel than it had initially, you will be required to pay inflated fuel prices. Be aware that the gas stations nearest airports are particularly expensive.

Driving in Florida

Driving in Florida is an efficient way to get around urban areas. It's also very straightforward: most highways are well-paved, gasoline is relatively inexpensive, and car rental rates are among the lowest in the US.

While there are many state and federal regulations on the equipment requirements of cars, there are very few that pertain to occupants. You must have a valid driver's license, and drivers and passengers can be fined for not wearing seatbelts. At certain times of the year state-wide campaigns make violations particularly expensive.

Parking

Finding a parking space is rarely a problem in Miami and the Keys, apart from near city beaches.

You will find small and multi-level parking lots or parking garages in cities, but usually you will have to use parking meters. Feed the meter generously: the fee varies from 50¢ to $2 per hour. Overstay and you risk a fine or your car being clamped or towed. Many parking meters can now be topped up using a smartphone.

Be sure to read parking signs carefully. Restrictions may be posted on telephone poles, street lights, or roadside walls. Cars parked within 10 ft (3 m) of a fire hydrant may be towed.

Roads and Tolls

Florida has an excellent road network. The fastest and smoothest routes are the interstate highways, which usually have six lanes and regular rest areas. They are referred to with names such as "I-10" and "I-75". Interstates form part of the expressway system of roads (sometimes called "freeways").

The major Interstates that lead to Miami are I-95 down the north coast, and I-75 from the Gulf Coast. There is also Florida's Turnpike, which is a toll road shooting down from Central Florida. The toll you have to pay is dependent on the distance covered. Tolls can be paid to a collector in a booth or – if you have the correct change and do not need a receipt – dropped into a collecting bin. Note that most sections of the Turnpike have been converted to an electronic system and cash is no longer accepted. Tolls are collected via **SunPass** transponders or from having your license plate photographed at each toll booth; your rental car agency can provide information on this.

State Roads and County Roads are smaller but better for casual touring by car. Unpaved routes exist in some of Florida's more rural areas; note that some car rental companies may not permit you to drive on these.

SunPass
W sunpass.com

Breakdown Assistance

If your car breaks down, pull off the road, turn on the emergency flashers, and wait for the police. On expressways you can make use of one of the Motorist Aid Call Boxes. If you have rented a car, you will find an emergency number on the rental agreement. The American Automobile Association **(AAA)** will assist its members. Alternatively, call the Florida Highway Patrol (511) or the Road Ranger service (*347).

AAA
W aaa.com

Rules of the Road

Drive on the right-hand side of the road. Seat belts are compulsory for both drivers and passengers.

Drinking and driving is illegal. Driving under the influence can result in a fine, having your driver's license suspended, or even imprisonment.

Passing is allowed on both sides on any multilane road, including interstate highways. It is illegal to change lanes across a double yellow or double white solid line. If a school bus stops on a two-way road to drop off or pick up children, traffic traveling in both directions must stop. On a divided highway, only traffic traveling in the same direction need stop.

Cycling

Cycling is a good way to get around South Beach, Key Biscayne, and Key West, but is not recommended elsewhere in Miami, where cars dominate. **CitiBike** has rental stations in Miami Beach, while **BikeMan Bike Rentals** offers eight locations in Key West.

For longer excursions, there are miles of marked cycle paths along the coast, including the Florida Keys Overseas Heritage Trail, which runs along US–1 to Key West.

BikeMan Bike Rentals
W bikemanbikerentalkeywest.com

CitiBike
W citibikemiami.com

Walking

Miami is pedestrian-friendly and walking is one of the most enjoyable ways to get around, particularly around the beaches.

Other Florida towns are not as walkable, especially in the hot and humid summers. But outside urban areas, the state has some lovely hikes. The **Florida Trail Association** provides information, including maps.

Florida Trail Association
W floridatrail.org

PRACTICAL INFORMATION

A little local know-how goes a long way in Miami and the Keys. On these pages you can find all the essential information you will need to make the most of your visit to the region.

AT A GLANCE

CURRENCY
Dollars (USD)

AVERAGE DAILY SPEND

SAVE	SPEND	SPLURGE
$50	$100	$300+

BOTTLED WATER	COFFEE	BEER	DINNER FOR TWO
$1.50	$4	$8	$100

CLIMATE

Summers are long, hot, and fairly humid. Temperatures in July hit 82°F (28°C).

Winters are mild. Temperatures can sink to 61°F (16°C) in January.

Short, sharp downpours are the norm in the wet season (May–Sep). Hurricane season is from June to November.

ELECTRICITY SUPPLY

The standard US electric current is 110 volts and 60 Hz. Power sockets are type A and B, fitting plugs with two flat pins.

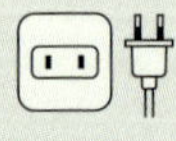

Passports and Visas

For entry requirements, including visas, consult your nearest US embassy or check with the **US Department of State**. All travelers to the US should have a passport that is valid for six months longer than their intended period of stay. Citizens of the UK, Australia, New Zealand, and the EU do not require visas for visits shorter than 90 days, but must apply to enter in advance via the Electronic System for Travel Authorization **(ESTA).** Applications must be made at least 72 hours before departure. Note that US entry requirements are incredibly volatile and are subject to change with little notice.

ESTA
W esta.cbp.dhs.gov
US Department of State
W travel.state.gov

Government Advice

Now more than ever, it is important to consult both your and the US government's advice before traveling. The US Department of State, the **UK Foreign, Commonwealth & Development Office (FCDO)**, and the **Australian Department of Foreign Affairs and Trade** offer the latest information on security, health, and local regulations.

Florida is occasionally at risk from hurricanes. Advance warnings are activated if there is any danger and **Ready** lists safety precautions.

Australian Department of Foreign Affairs and Trade
W smartraveller.gov.au
Ready
W ready.gov/hurricanes
UK Foreign, Commonwealth & Development Office (FCDO)
W gov.uk/foreign-travel-advice

Customs Information

You can find information on the laws relating to goods and currency taken in or out of the US on the **Customs and Border Protection Agency** website. All travelers need to complete a Customs and Border Protection Agency form.

Customs and Border Protection Agency
W cbp.gov

Insurance

We recommend that you take out a comprehensive insurance policy covering theft, loss of belongings, medical care, cancellations and delays, and read the small print carefully. All medical treatment is private; US health insurers do not have reciprocal arrangements with other countries.

Money

The currency is the US dollar ($), made up of 100 cents (¢). Bills (notes) come in denominations of $1, $5, $10, $20, $50, and $100, while coins are 1¢ (usually called a penny), 5¢ (nickel), 10¢ (dime), 25¢ cents (quarter) and, rarely, 50¢ (half-dollar), and one dollar.

Most establishments accept major credit, debit, and prepaid currency cards. Contactless payments are common, but cash is usually required for smaller items and tips. You should always tip service industry workers. Waiters and taxi drivers will expect to be tipped 15 per cent of the total bill.

Travelers with Specific Requirements

US law demands that all public buildings be accessible to people in wheelchairs. A number of groups offer advice for travelers with disabilities, including **Mobility International USA**. **Visit Florida Keys** provides island-specific advice, with useful tips on boats and ferries, and the **Florida Disabled Outdoors Association** lists activities throughout the state. **Miami Lighthouse for the Blind and Visually Impaired** has been running events, services and programs for the visually impaired for decades, and remains an important community for Miami's visually impaired residents and their families.

When it comes to getting around, most city buses are able to "kneel" to make access easier – look for a sticker on the windshield or by the door. Many of Miami's sidewalks are narrow and congested, which can pose a problem for some wheelchair users. A few car rental companies, including **Wheelchair Getaways**, have vehicles that are adapted for people with disabilities.

Florida Disabled Outdoors Association
W fdoa.org

Miami Lighthouse for the Blind and Visually Impaired
W miamilighthouse.org

Mobility International USA
W miusa.org

Visit Florida Keys
W fla-keys.com/travelers-with-disabilities

Wheelchair Getaways
W wheelchairgetaways.com

Language

The official language of Florida is English, but parts of Miami are home to large Latin American communities, where Spanish is also spoken.

Opening Hours

The majority of shops are open 9am–6pm Monday–Saturday and noon–6pm Sunday, but be aware that times can differ considerably between cities and rural areas. Most museums and tourist sights in South Florida and Miami are open daily, although they may close on either Monday or Tuesday. Many local businesses and attractions close on federal and state holidays.

Situations can change quickly and unexpectedly. Always check before visiting attractions and hospitality venues for up-to-date opening hours and booking requirements.

Personal Security

Florida is a relatively safe place to visit, but it is still advisable to take precautions. As in any urban area, there are parts of Miami where you should stay alert. Plan your routes in advance, look at maps discreetly, walk with confidence, and be cautious in deserted areas. If you need directions, ask hotel or shop staff, or the police.

Make sure your credit cards, cell phone, and cash are kept in a safe place. If you have anything stolen, report the crime as soon as possible to the nearest police station. Get a copy of the crime report in order to claim on your insurance. Most credit card companies have toll-free numbers for reporting a loss.

Contact your embassy or consulate as well as the police if you have your passport stolen. In the event of a serious crime or accident, call the **emergency number.**

As a rule, Floridians are accepting of all people, regardless of their race, gender, or sexuality, though the state has become increasingly politically divided under the current administration. Many locals in Miami pride themselves on their progressive values, but the same can't always be said for the population in wider Florida. The state has a big Latin American and African American population, and debates have raged in recent years over the removal of confederate statues and the renaming of historic streets, buildings, and squares.

Miami and the Keys have a long history as LGBTQ+-friendly vacation destinations. This attitude, however, is rarer in the state's more rural areas. If you do feel unsafe, the **Safe Space Alliance** pinpoints your nearest place of refuge.

Emergency Number
W 911

Safe Space Alliance
W safespacealliance.com

Health

Healthcare in the US is excellent but can be very costly. Ensure you have full medical coverage prior to your visit, and keep all receipts to claim on your insurance if needed. Hospitals accept the majority of credit cards, as do most doctors and dentists. Those without insurance may need to pay in advance.

AT A GLANCE

EMERGENCY NUMBERS

GENERAL EMERGENCY

911

TIME ZONE

EST (Eastern Standard Time - except for Panhandle - CST - Central Standard Time).

TAP WATER

Unless otherwise stated, tap water in Florida is safe to drink.

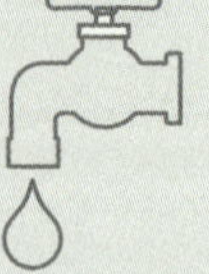

WEBSITES AND APPS

Miami's tourist board
visitmiami.com

Florida's tourist board
visitflorida.com

National Hurricane Center
nhc.noaa.gov

American Automobile Association
aaa.com

The US rail network
amtrak.com

America's national bus network
greyhound.com

Most hospitals in Miami and further south towards the Keys offer first-class healthcare, though hospitals outside of the city are smaller and will likely have fewer appointments times.

Smoking, Alcohol, and Drugs

Florida has a partial smoking ban, with lighting up prohibited in most spaces and on public transportation. Users of e-cigarettes follow the same rules.

You must be over 21 to buy and drink alcohol, and to buy tobacco products. It is advisable to carry valid ID at all times, as you will not be permitted to enter bars or order alcoholic beverages in restaurants without it.

Local Customs

Tipping is an important custom in Florida, as in the rest of the US. Anyone who provides a service expects to receive a "gratuity", and this needs to be calculated in the price of things like meals, hotel stays, and taxi journeys.

Responsible Travel

It is relatively easy to travel sustainably within Miami, which has an increasing number of eco-conscious restaurants and hotels and a reliable public transportation network. Many locals choose to cycle or roller skate along the waterfront to avoid the city's congested roads. Ensure you leave no trace when enjoying the beach, as litter can become a major problem in the tourist season.

As the climate crisis worsens, it is increasingly important that visitors respect the delicate subtropical and marine ecosystems of the Keys and the Everglades. Where possible, try to book tours with an environmentally responsible organizer. Ensure you admire all wildlife from a safe distance, and respect signs advising you against swimming in certain waters.

Cell Phones and Wi-Fi

Triband or multiband cell phones from around the world should work in the US, but your service provider may have to unlock international roaming. It is worth checking this with your provider before you set off.

Even if your phone does work, you'll need to be particularly careful about roaming charges, especially for data, which can be extortionate. It can be much cheaper to buy a US SIM card ($10 or less) to use during your stay (you can also buy micro-SIMs, nano-SIMs or the increasingly popular e-SIMS, available via phone apps). Some networks also sell basic phones (with free minutes) for as little as $30 (no paperwork or ID is required). The main network providers are AT&T, Sprint, T-Mobile US, and Verizon.

To make any call in Miami, even next door, you must dial the 305 area code, but not the 1 before it. The **Directory Assistance** is a useful service for finding telephone numbers.

Free Wi-Fi is ubiquitous in Miami. Most hotels, hostels, and coffee shops offer Wi-Fi, and there are several Wi-Fi hotspots scattered throughout the city.

Directory Assistance
T 411

Postal Services

The **United States Postal Service** operates Florida's postal services. The most comprehensive post offices are Miami Beach Post Office on Washington Avenue and Key West Post Office on Whitehead Street. Stamps are sold in many drugstores, hotels, and grocery stores. All US domestic mail goes first class, and you should use airmail for any overseas mail. Rates are currently $1.65 for letters to all international destinations.

United States Postal Service
W usps.com

Taxes

The state sales tax in Florida is 6 per cent. Local authorities can add additional levies up to a maximum 2.5 per cent. Miami adds 1 per cent.

PLACES TO STAY

Miami is deservedly famous for its abundance of glamorous waterfront hotels, many designed in the city's signature Tropical Deco style. Those looking to spend a pretty dollar will find the ultimate in luxury throughout the city and across the Keys. But there are also a good handful of humble hostels and cheaper resorts tucked between the higher-end offerings. Note that prices rise dramatically during the summer, and accommodation can be hard to secure during Spring Break (late March to early April).

PRICE CATEGORIES

For a standard, double room per night (with breakfast if included), with taxes and extra charges.

$ under $160
$$ $160–$450
$$$ over $450

Miami Beach

1 Hotel South Beach

S1 2341 Collins Ave
1hotels.com · $$$

The original outpost of this ultra-exclusive chain, 1 Hotel South Beach opened in the heart of SoBe in 2015. With marble floors, a grand lobby, and countless supercars in the entryway, the hotel offers the perfect induction into Miami chic – before you even reach your suite. But alongside its luxury trappings, 1 Hotel also appeases the eco-conscious, with tastefully recycled furnishings, wooden keys, and LED lights throughout.

Loews Miami Beach

S3 1601 Collins Ave, South Beach loewshotels.com/miami-beach · $$$

The vast estate of Loews is like Miami in microcosm. Within, you'll find a boutique mall, swimming pool, spa, gym, and private beach. There's even an uber-popular iteration of New York's Rao's Neapolitan restaurant on site. But before you discover this buzzing world inside, you'll notice the hotel's facade: Loews is housed in SoBe's tallest Art Deco tower, making it a celebrated icon of the beachfront.

SLS South Beach

S2 1701 Collins Ave
slshotels.com/south-beach · $$$

Arriving into a hotel lobby on a red carpet speaks volumes about the experience you'll find within. Miami has a long list of hip stays, but few offer "over the top VIP beachfront luxury" – their words – quite like SLS. Sip Manhattans with liquid cherries in the bustling Bar Central, tuck into elevated Caribbean dishes at Cartagena restaurant, and party at the exclusive Hyde Beach, before retiring to your ocean-facing suite. Downtime doesn't come more indulgent than this.

Cardozo South Beach

S3 1300 Ocean Dr
cardozohotel.com · $

Screen travelers rejoice. Having appeared in an array of big-screen hits, including *Something About Mary* (1998), the Cardozo has all the cinematic pedigree of more esteemed Art Deco hotels for a fraction of the cost. Built in 1939, the hotel is now owned by Gloria and Emilio Estefan, who have transformed an ageing institution into a modern success, with chic rooms flaunting all-white decor.

Avalon

S4 700 Ocean Dr
avalonhotel.com · $$

Miami Beach has more Art Deco buildings than anywhere in the US, but few are as celebrated as the Avalon. Dating back to 1941, the hotel was designed by world-renowned architect Albert Anis, a pioneer of Miami's Tropical Deco style. Recognize that green-hued exterior? The Avalon has appeared in such local classics as *Miami Vice* (1984) and *Scarface* (1983). Located in the middle of SoBe's most popular stretch, the hotel has every amenity you could hope for, from superb room service to a well-stocked cocktail bar.

Esmé Miami Beach

S3 1438 Washington Ave esmehotel.com · $

Tucked down Española Way – once the storied haunt of Spanish movie stars, Cuban fashionistas, and hustlers of all stripes – Esmé leans into its Latin American history. With its striped awnings and al-fresco terrace seating, the hotel evokes the nostalgic comfort of a Mediterranean holiday while celebrating Miami's own Hispanic past. Inside, artfully furnished, mid-century retro rooms offer comfort without breaking the bank.

Essex House

S4 1001 Collins Ave essexhotel.com · $

With its sister hotel the Clevelander set just next door, Essex House essentially offers the amenities of two hotels in one. Guests aged 21 years and over have access to the huge pool and patio, but the hotel's main draw is its prime location near SoBe's bustling nightclubs and restaurants. You're just a short walk from the city's most dynamic ocean-facing attractions, too, making for a convenient and comparatively affordable stay in a pricey area.

Fontainebleau, Miami Beach

H3 4441 Collins Ave fontainebleau.com · $$$

For over seven decades, Fontainebleau has epitomized Miami luxury. Stay here and you'll join an esteemed lineage of celebrity icons, from Frank Sinatra to Lady Gaga. No expense has been spared in ensuring the hotel offers the pinnacle of glamour: rooms are large, many with amazing views, and there is a luxury pool complex, the perfect place for A-lister spotting. Many come for the huge spa, which offers pampering of the highest order.

The Standard

H3 4441 Collins Ave standardhotels.com · $$$

The owners of The Standard would rather you didn't call this a "hotel", preferring "adults-only spa with guest rooms". Walk in, and you'll quickly see why. The entire space is expertly crafted to induce deep relaxation. There are the hot tubs on the terrace outside every room; there's the huge hydrotherapy center teaching ancient bathing customs; there are the swaying palm trees in the tropical garden, with professional yogis humming mantras in their shade. The only danger here is snapping out of your reverie when it's time to leave.

Hotel Gaythering

Q2 1409 Lincoln Rd, South Beach gaythering.com · $

Catering exclusively to LGBTQ+ guests, Hotel Gaythering proudly declares itself the "gayest venue in Miami Beach". The legendary Gaythering Bar hosts an array of riotous events, including karaoke and bingo (though not as you've ever played it before). There's also a large spa, renowned as Miami's most exciting. Needless to say, perhaps don't choose Gaythering if you're looking for a quiet holiday.

Downtown and Little Havana

W Miami

N3 485 Brickell Ave wmiamihotel.com · $$$

W Miami enlisted some of the biggest names in architecture and design – including American interior designer Kelly Wearstler – to create Downtown's most glamorous stay. A particular highlight is the sophisticated contemporary cuisine on offer at the hotel's TULUM restaurant, best enjoyed on the sprawling roof terrace.

EAST Miami

N3 788 Brickell Plaza
east-miami.com · $$

Offering sophisticated, no-frills luxury, this plush hotel in the heart of Downtown is as popular with business people as it is with holidaying families. EAST has perfected the familiar blueprint of the upscale stay, with its large and minimalist rooms, sleek corridors, and excellent room service.

Kimpton Epic

N3 788 Brickell Plaza
epichotel.com/downtown-miami-spa ·$$

Exercise fanatic? Kimpton Epic is for you. This wellness hotel is home to a state-of-the-art fitness center housed in a 54-story tower, so you can work up a sweat with sweeping views. Through the concierge, you'll have first dibs on an array of adrenaline-inducing experiences across the city, from speedboat rides to kayak adventures. Epic indeed.

North of Downtown

The Breakers

D2 1 South County Rd, Palm Beach thebreakers.com · $$$

An icon of Palm Beach, The Breakers stands as an enduring testament to the vision of its founder, the industrialist Henry M. Flagler. While the hotel preserves his grand Spanish Revival style and ornate furnishings, it has evolved with the times, marrying 19th-century opulence with modern conveniences like sustainable bath products, accessible rooms, and a personal concierge service.

Four Seasons Resort Palm Beach

D2 2800 South Ocean Blvd, Palm Beach
fourseasons.com · $$$

When it comes to a memorable stay, sometimes the small gestures matter just as much as the grand: bowls of fresh fruit in the lobby, orchids in the bedroom, a doorman who remembers your name. At the Four Seasons, now globally synonymous with luxury, these tiny touches seem effortless. Here, it's just great service all the way down.

The Ritz-Carlton Fort Lauderdale

D3 1 N Fort Lauderdale Beach Blvd
ritzcarlton.com · $$$

Overlooking the beach, this popular hotel features a world-class restaurant, a huge spa, a heated infinity pool, and a top-notch fitness center. When you're finally ready to leave these amenities and explore, you're right on a trolley line, providing a free ride to Las Olas and other local attractions.

Hollywood Beach Suites & Hotel

D3 334 Arizona St
hollywoodbeachsuitehotel.com · $

Just a minute's walk from Hollywood Beach and Broadwalk, this humble retreat is a popular choice for ocean lovers of all stripes. With kayaks and other seafaring equipment available to borrow, you'll hardly want to leave the beach; you can even eat at the on-site Taco Beach Shack.

Grandview Gardens

D2 1608 Lake Ave, West Palm Beach
grandview-gardens.com · $$

Set on a charming block amid tropical gardens, this tranquil property features classic Spanish Mediterranean style, an outdoor pool, and large period rooms. As you emerge onto the palm-shaded terrace as the sun sets, cocktail in hand, you won't believe how close you are to the energy and bustle of Palm Beach.

Cabanas Guesthouse & Spa

D3 2209 NE 26th St, Wilton Manors thecabanasguesthouse.com · $$

Set in Wilton Manors, Fort Lauderdale's gay district, this boutique hotel has an all-male day spa, two pools, and a clothing-optional jacuzzi set amid lush gardens.

Many hotels claim to be relaxing; by all accounts, this one truly means it.

Coral Gables and Coconut Grove

Mayfair House Hotel & Garden

G3 3000 Florida Ave mayfairhotelmiami.com · $$$

A boutique hotel and lush tropical garden set atop a shopping mall? In Miami, anything goes. Here you'll find large suites with mahogany furniture, marble baths, and spacious balconies. And for a spot of retail therapy, you won't even need to venture outside.

The Biltmore

F3 1200 Anastasia Ave biltmore hotel.com · $$$

Since opening in 1926, this icon has smashed countless world records: once the tallest building in Florida (thanks to the spiraling Spanish Giralda Tower) it still houses the largest hotel swimming pool in the US. The entire building is so iconic, in fact, that it has been designated a National Historic Landmark *(p107)*.

Mr. C Coconut Grove

F3 2988 McFarlane Road mrccoconutgrove.com · $$

Owned by the legendary Cipriani family, who run a network of hospitality venues across Florida, this hotel provides Italian luxury with a Floridian twist, in the historic neighborhood of Coconut Grove.

Hotel St. Michel

G3 162 Alcazar Ave, at Ponce de Leon Blvd, Coral Gables hotel stmichel.com · $

Harking back to 1926, the heyday of George Merrick's architectural vision, Hotel St. Michel is among the most recognizable spots in Coral Gables – and there are many. A long legacy is not enough to sustain a modern hotel, so Hotel St. Michel has adapted with the times, offering a well-stocked gym and modern rooms accented with beautiful antiques.

South of Coconut Grove

Hoosville Hostel

E6 20 SW 2nd Ave, Florida City hoos ville hostel.com · $

This hostel's amenities include a waterfall pool and a fire pit – but with the Everglades so close, you'll find it hard to spend much time here. Hoosville offers everything you could possibly need for a wild adventure.

The Keys

Seashell Motel & Key West Hostel

A6 718 South St, Key West keywest hostel.com · $

A trip to Key West needn't be expensive when gems like Seashell exist. Combining a friendly motel with a hostel for larger groups or solo travelers, here you can book snorkeling trips or scuba lessons, rent bikes, or simply kick back in the sunny picnic area and game rooms. There are only ten private rooms, so advance booking is strongly advised.

Hawks Cay Resort

MAP B6 61 Hawks Cay Blvd, Duck Key hawkscay.com · $$$

This exclusive Keys resort offers every watersport you could hope to try (and a few you may never have heard of): fishing, offshore sailing, scuba diving, snorkeling, parasailing, kayaking, water-skiing, glass-bottom boat tours, you name it.

Deer Run on the Atlantic

B6 1997 Long Beach Rd, Big Pine Key deerrunontheatlantic.com · $$

Sustainable initiatives might have become more common in Florida's hotels, but few are as holistically green as Deer Run. This entirely vegan and organic institution is situated next to a pristine beach, a perfect place for a mindful and restorative retreat. The best bit? The myriad vegan delights whipped up by Chef Gail Patak.

INDEX

Page numbers in **bold** refer to main entries.

D

E

F

G

H

I

ACKNOWLEDGMENTS

This edition updated by

Contributor Toni DeBella

Senior Editors Keith Drew, Dipika Dasgupta

Senior Designers Stuti Tiwari, Katie Cavanagh

Project Art Editor Bharti Karakoti

Project Editor Alex Pathe

Editors Nandini Desiraju, Vineet Singh

Deputy Picture Research Manager Virien Chopra

Rights and Permissions Specialist Vagisha Pushp

Assistant Picture Research Administrator Manpreet Kaur

Publishing Assistant Simona Velikova

Jacket Designer Laura O'Brien

Jacket Picture Researcher Simona Velikova

Senior Cartographer Subhashree Bharati

Cartography Manager Suresh Kumar

Senior Executive Cartographic Editor James Macdonald

Pre-Production Coordinator Tanveer Zaidi

Pre-Production Designer Rohit Rojal

Production Controller Kariss Ainsworth

Deputy Managing Editor Dharini Ghanesh

Managing Editor Beverly Smart

Managing Art Editor Gemma Doyle

Senior Managing Art Editor Priyanka Thakur

Editorial Director Hollie Teague

Art Director Maxine Pedliham

Publishing Director Georgina Dee

DK would like to thank the following for their contribution to the previous editions: Megan Eaves, Hilary Bird, Susanne Hillen, Stephen Keeling, Jeffrey Kennedy, Patrick Peterson.

The publisher would like to thank the following for their kind permission to reproduce their photographs:

Key: a-above; b-below/bottom; c-center; f-far; l-left; r-right; t-top

4Corners: Pietro Canali 45; Susanne Kremer 33

Adobe Stock: Jillian Cain 53b; Earth Pixel LLC. 1, 5, 6–7, 12crb; lazyllama 16cr; Zenstratus 40–41t.

Alamy Stock Photo: Allen Creative / Steve Allen 75; James Anderson 76; Associated Press / Pete Wright 10cl; Marcus Baker 23cb; Cavan Images 61; Sergey Chernyaev 13clb, 113; Chronicle / Mary Evans Picture Library 8; Ian Dagnall 15tl; Walter Bibikow / DanitaDelimont.com 134t; Danita Delimont 41b, 63b, 134–135b; Earth Pixel LLC 17, 25b, 27, 60; FL Stock 122; Zachary Frank 43br; Godong 49t; Luis Gomez 12cr, 22; Chris Gug 59; Soularue / Hemis.fr 87; Horizon International Images 86; imageBROKER / Marc Rasmus 130; Jeffrey Isaac Greenberg 1+ 91; Jeffrey Isaac Greenberg 2+ 103; Jeffrey Isaac Greenberg 3+ 51b; Jeffrey Isaac Greenberg 4+ 90, 119; Jeffrey Isaac Greenberg 7+ 78b; Jeffrey Isaac Greenberg 8+ 26t, 57, 72t, 99; Jeffrey Isaac Greenberg 10+ 23bl; Jeffrey Isaac Greenberg 12+ 112; Jeffrey Isaac Greenberg 16+ 34, 72b; Jeffrey Isaac Greenberg 18+ 35b, 48; John Kellerman 11; Terry Kelly 79; Carver Mostardi 115; Mpi04 / Media Punch 68–69b; Nikreates 108–109t, 111; NiKreative 51t; Nathaniel Noir 29br, 73t; North Wind Picture Archives 9tl; PA Images / Yui Mok 69t; Wiliam Perry 94; Prisma by Dukas Presseagentur GmbH / Heeb Christian 123; Yaroslav Sabitov / YES Market Media 66; Tom Salyer 21t; James Schwabel 42, 64, 67b; SOPA Images 10bl; Stephen Saks Photography 29bl; Tom Stack 13cl (8); State Archives of Florida / Florida Memory 10tl; Charles Stirling (Travel) 133; Cheryl Acrey / Stockimo 73b; Mark Summerfield 136; Island Syndicate 39t; James Talalay 116; The Book Worm 9tr; The Granger Collection 9cra; WorldPix 117; WS Collection 9br.

AWL Images: Susanne Kremer 12br, 19.

Bal Harbour Shops: 74.

Courtesy of Vizcaya Museum and Gardens Archives: Bill Sumner 31.

Depositphotos Inc: PeterEtchells 52–53t.

Dreamstime.com: Francisco Blanco 20cra, 62, 95; Bluiz60 56; Ciolca 46; Brett Critchley 55b; Demerzel21 / Holocaust Memorial in Miami Beach, Florida, USA 47b; Fotoluminate 32; Giovanni Gagliardi 13tl, 63t; Jorgeinthewater 16cla; Kmiragaya 50, 65b; Mariakray 84–85; Meinzahn 15b, 24, 30; Christian Ouellet 121; Sean Pavone 39b; Vadim Rodnev 20clb; Romrodinka 54; Alexander Shapovalov 118; Oleksandr Shyripa 71b; Studiobarcelona 26b; TasFoto 38; Tifonimages 25t; Damien Verrier 77b; Viavaltours 14; Ken Wolter 13bl; Xbrchx 96.

Florida Keys News Bureau: Bob Care 126; Stephen Frink 58; Bob Krist 127; Andy Newman 129.

Getty Images: Bettmann 10br; Moment / Carlos Carreno 125; Moment / Joe Daniel Price 92;

Moment / YuriF 13cl; Jason Koerner / Stringer 71t; Alexander Tamargo 70; Thaddaeus McAdams / WireImage 89; The Chronicle Collection / Ray Fisher 47t.

Getty Images / iStock: ampueroleonardo 67t; Boogich 88; CircleEyes 43bl; E+ / lavin photography 124; E+ / Torresigner 139; travelview 68t; Flavio Vallenari 55t.

Provided by the Greater Miami Convention & Visitors Bureau www.gmcvb.com: Cris Ascunce 29cb.

Inn on Fifth: 137.

Jalan Jalan: 104.

The Kampong: 108b.

Little Havana Tours: 12cra, 28.

Mandolin Aegean Bistro: 105.

Miami Dade College: Cristian Lazzari 78t.

Pérez Art Museum Miami: east façade February 2014 Designed by Herzog & de Meuron Photo by Armando Colls/MannyofMiami.com 97.

The Phillip and Patricia Frost Museum of Science: Ra-Haus 65t, 93.

Shutterstock.com: Marco Borghini 107; Cavan-Images 16cl; Dmitry Tkachenko Photo 81; Jason Heid 43crb; JTTucker 131; Mayskyphoto 83; Mia2you 13cla, 101; Nikkibry 21b; Sergio TB 15cra; Stillgravity 110; Whispering Willow Images 16tc.

University of Miami Lowe Art Museum: 35t.

The Wolfsonian - Florida International University: 37tl; TD1988.34.1- Stained glass window, commissioned 1926, completed 1930 (never installed) For the International Labor Building, League of Nations, Geneva / The Mitchell Wolfson Jr. Collection 36; TD1991.36.1 - Wrestler: Sculpture, Wrestler, 1929, Dudley Vaill Talcott (American, 1899–1986), Shown at the Tenth Olympic Games, Los Angeles, CA, 1932, Aluminum / The Mitchell Wolfson Jr. Collection 37tr; XX1989.429 -Window grille, 1929 From the Norris Theatre, Norristown, Pennsylvania Architects: William Harold Lee (American, 1884–1971) and Armand Carroll (American, 1898–1976) Manufacturer: ConklingArmstrong Terra Cotta Company, Philadelphia Glazed terra cotta, / The Mitchell Wolfson Jr. Collection 37ca.

Wynwood Walls: Martha Cooper 49b, 77t; DRIK (artist) / Nika Kramer (photographer) 102.

Cover images:

Front and Spine: **Getty Images:** Moment / Alexander Spatari; *Back:* **Adobe Stock:** Earth Pixel LLC. cl; **Alamy Stock Photo:** Earth Pixel LLC tl, James Schwabel tr.

Pull out map:

Getty Images: Moment / Alexander Spatari.

A NOTE FROM DK

The rate at which the world is changing is constantly keeping the DK travel team on our toes. While we've worked hard to ensure that this edition of Miami and the Keys is accurate, we know that opening hours alter, standards shift, prices fluctuate, places close and new ones pop up in their stead. So, if you notice we've got something wrong or left something out, we want to hear about it. Please get in touch at travelguides@dk.com

Within each Top 10 list in this book, no hierarchy of quality or popularity is implied. All 10 are, in the editor's opinion, of roughly equal merit.

First edition 2005

Published in Great Britain by Dorling Kindersley Limited, DK, 20 Vauxhall Bridge Road, London SW1V 2SA

The authorised representative in the EEA is Dorling Kindersley Verlag GmbH. Arnulfstr. 124, 80636 Munich, Germany

Published in the United States by DK Publishing, 1745 Broadway, 20th Floor, New York, NY 10019, USA

25 26 27 28 10 9 8 7 6 5 4 3 2 1

A CIP catalog record for this book is available from the British Library.

A catalog record for this book is available from the Library of Congress.

ISSN: 1479-344X
ISBN: 978 0 2417 5761 1

Printed and bound in China

www.dk.com

MIX
Paper | Supporting responsible forestry
FSC™ C018179

This book was made with Forest Stewardship Council™ certified paper – one small step in DK's commitment to a sustainable future.

Learn more at **www.dk.com/uk/information/sustainability**